Transformation

Transformation

Channelled by
JULIE SOSKIN

Published by
The College of Psychic Studies
16 Queensberry Place, London, SW7 2EB

First published in 1995 by
The College of Psychic Studies
16 Queensberry Place, London, SW7 2EB

British Library Cataloguing-in-Publication Data

A catalogue record of this book
is available from The British Library
ISBN 0 903336 24 3

Typeset, printed and bound in Great Britain
by Whitstable Litho, Whitstable, Kent.

Contents

Acknowledgements

Much appreciation and thanks go to my dear friend Gwenie who serenely sat with me throughout the channelling of this book; to my patient and wonderful family; and to life for all its many opportunities.

Note: Throughout this book, the references to 'man' and 'he' are used in a collective sense to describe all of humanity. They have no preference and recognise no superiority of gender.

Foreword

It was in 1989, bombarded by information of vast world changes, that the channelling began. Six years have elapsed since then, and so much has happened on all levels it is almost impossible to keep track.

People are expanding in their consciousness extraordinarily quickly. Intuitive awareness has arrived into common consciousness and much of my work now is in helping the process of spiritual integration into the material world, helping to open up intuitive areas in the mind, so we can all finally come into our own power.

A question often asked is, "Who is the channelling from?" When the channelling began the answer we were given was, "a unison of light forces – original thought". So what are these light forces and what or who is original thought?

Whilst channelling, I feel as if I am locked into a beam, aware of speaking but rarely remembering the words. This is why sessions are recorded and someone always sits with me. The channelling is devoid of personality but feels very loving. My own mind is being used but some of the information is beyond my normal intelligence. There is a realisation of not being alone but no feeling of individuality. I have often pondered therefore on how best to answer this question.

Perhaps the honest answer is that it is the highest self, for what is our highest self, if not the god part of man? Perhaps tongue in cheek the reply should be that it comes from God. Unfortunately there would be some who would take it literally! Far too many people are only too happy to give away their power. However, whatever it is, it does seem to be able to access information beyond the normal sources. I can therefore only do my bit as the medium, to the best of my ability, and hope that the words offer inspiration and comfort.

Too many people are carried away by information either because of the charisma of the medium or the name of the channelled entity. What most people do not realise is that it is very easy for a mischievous lower entity to masquerade as a higher soul. If the words ring true, listen, but be very discerning; it is not the time to give away your power, but rather it is time to reclaim it. If in any doubt, walk away. The reality is that everyone can receive higher forces and higher information if they choose to listen for themselves.

We have recently been told that channelling is not so much about receiving words, but more about accessing higher consciousness. Channelling creates the opening to 'greater possibilities', allowing the flow of energy to a higher force, and channelling will decrease as more and more people are able to access this for themselves.

Unlike my previous books, Transformation was channelled over a longer period of time running between June 1993 and July 1994. My dear friend Gwenie sat with me throughout and we initially contacted a group energy, mainly for our own purposes. These I affectionately call 'The Professors'. This group is contacted through the higher astral planes, but in itself is not an astral energy. It uses the higher astral as a passage to many who are still awakening. It is an amalgamation of light beings attracted together for humanity's expansion and it is often present in individual sittings as they can relate to the individual. This body of beings, from many different places and times, seems to be very active, helping to expand consciousness and guide us through the difficult transition. These initial sessions had a different energy to the rest of the channelling but they have been included as Chapter One because they offered some interesting information about group work at this time. Very often after these sessions we had an intense feeling of connection and peace. It really is 'the peace that passes all understanding'. We always felt uplifted and mentally and spiritually stretched.

Many people, including myself, have experienced accelerated shifts of consciousness which this book seems to mirror. The shift spoken of in the last chapter was for me, perhaps, the most startling: in full waking consciousness I observed the universe, becoming part of the kaleidoscope of the cosmos. I saw the countless stars and galaxies, wheels and colours, flowing gracefully, constantly moving, changing colour and shape, on and on, without end. Our planet Earth, a tiny, tiny speck, and the negative energy that gives so much concern was nothing. The whole universe changed colour and shape a thousand, thousand times. The huge wonder of this was almost too overwhelming to bear.

After this experience I was left with an empty feeling. Not in a pessimistic way, but as a reality. It made me reassess my life, my work I asked myself, what was I doing? What could possibly be worthwhile when everything will change, move, dissolve, only to form again and again in endless, continuous patterns.

Most of us have asked the question, "What is the meaning of life?" Perhaps life has no other purpose than to be, to experience. The growth is just a by-product of this. What I do know is that most of us waste time on too many irrelevances – but even they have colour!

Since we have all chosen to be here, all any of us can do is live each day in truth, embracing the rich kaleidoscope of colours, knowing we are all part of the cosmos and ultimately part of each and everything.

For myself and many others, having felt the lower base energies in the body dissolve many years ago, it was somewhat of a surprise when, in the autumn of 1993, we felt the lower centres re-activate with a clearer force, strangely bringing us into a new balance of the higher and lower bodies. It felt as if the old energies had 'gone to the cleaners' and had come back sparkling and new. Many people are now using a different, clearer base force, clear of fear and ancient patterns. It has made us really appreciate the instrument of the body, our planet Earth, and the incredible balance and harmony of everything. Once an individual is in harmony and realises their alignment, wonderful perfect syncronicity occurs in all things, in all ways, and we can truly recognize the miracle of life.

As the channelling has said, "The time of learning through suffering is coming to an end; the time of learning through joy has begun".

Julie Soskin 1995

About the Author

Julie Soskin was born in the London suburb of Twickenham in 1952, and first became aware of her psychic abilities at the age of four. In her early 20's she began to develop these abilities. Eighteen months was spent in a spiritualist group, and she went on to do a further two years training with Elizabeth Farrell at the College of Psychic Studies in London.

Julie worked happily as a clairvoyant medium until, in 1989, a series of shifts of consciousness enabled her to contact the channelled connection with which she now works. This led to the publication of her three previous books, *Wind of Change, Cosmic Dance,* and *Alignment to Light.* All of these books speak of the changing times in which we live.

Julie now travels extensively, lecturing and assisting others with self-awareness, psychic development and higher consciousness. She feels the most important aspect of her work is to help others to be in touch with their intuition which is essential for the coming times.

Chapter 1

The Cosmic Professors

It is right that you make this time available for your own processing, your own deliverance and communication as well as for that of others. This link is firmly established from what you describe as the higher consciousness realm.

There are many helpers along the pathway, in different frequencies, different beings, different states, who help, depending on the individual's energy at any given time. We do not give a name because it is not relevant, appropriate or necessary.

But you need to know who we are. Let us just say we are a band of helpers, we have different energies and entities working within this band. These are dependent on the magnetism of the channeller, some of these entities are what you define as extraterrestrial beings, but that in itself is misleading because none of us clearly are within the physical body in any case. This band of helpers are in operation, automatically, with people all over the world, and though we can say we are here with you now as a group energy, we are also working with those in other parts of your world. Quite literally, at any moment, we are here and we are there. It is the energy frequency that the channeller can join with at this time, but the waves are open and anyone can communicate with us.

It is of great fascination to our cosmic brethren that we are doing this, they can assist with their knowledge of light bodies, and are of particular use when it comes to the redefining of their etheric frame.

We greet you with what you define as love. We greet you with friendship and we greet you with joy. We are, in your words, friendly.

There have always been guides and helpers on the different planes of existence to lead the way and to assist, most often without any recognition on the part of the practitioner. We are grateful for this communication because there is a purpose now in us being in contact for the good of others. Before we begin, we want to say – for the channeller's sake – that this communication is not separate from the higher consciousness channelling that she has observed, it is merely taking one facet of it so that we can speak individually with more, let us say, human terminology.

The purpose of this communication is to let you know that there is a huge movement within the processing work that is going on within the human body, mind, spirit and emotions. There is a high acceleration, which you all know about, because the energy frequency has hit the physical manifestation – the physical body. You are all observing things within yourselves that are, to put it mildly, unusual.

Doctors will observe the unusual cases they are getting. All those who work with people on a physical level will observe the change and some will put a title on it, or give it names. That is not relevant, because the changes we speak of are not static in themselves. It is not a case of change from A to B, or from A to Z. It is a fluid state of change.

There is a fluidity now within the cellular structure. It is not fixed or structured, it is still very much in that transitional process. It may be many years before it stabilises. Those who deal with blood, or those who look at the cells within blood will see this through their microscopes, wondering if some new disease or illness has infiltrated the human condition. There will be some consternation regarding this, and to begin with, it might be ignored but it is going to be impossible to ignore when it is in front of the human eye.

There will be some who fear that this is caused by your nuclear fall-outs – it is not. There will be organisations that will say, "See, this is what we told you. This is what we said. This is the danger of these things." It has nothing to do with it. It is just the change of the human existence

Muscles will react differently. We cannot say, because of its fluid state, where this will finish and how it will finally stabilise. But one thing is certain, it is with the evolutionary expansion of man himself. This will cause a shake-up of the reproductive areas, as much as any other organs, and although we cannot give a fixed condition, it is likely that the gender of human beings will be very much less defined in the future. Therefore, man will reach an androgynous state, or similar. But again we must emphasise this is fluid, although there are certain indications already as to how this is happening.

The development of the new man is being achieved through the etheric bodies and here, some our 'colleagues' help. But even they must go along with the fluidity, so the architecture of the etheric states cannot be fixed either, but moves so that the etheric angels can constantly re-adjust the energies because they are the ones most sensitive to them. When we speak of a new man (these phrases have been used before), we say to you we are literally talking about New Man. The body of man is now altering.

When this information of the new times started, it was easier in some ways to assess, to assimilate, because it was to do with the spiritual make-up and indeed it still is. But everything affects everything else, and the purpose of our communication is to set about the task of relieving fears within all of you who are so conscious now of the changes within the body.

If we had spoken even a few years ago about the transmutation of man in this way, it could have caused panic and you would have imagined some horror-state. But it is no horror, it is wondrous, because the body has to be able to accommodate the spiritual essence, the spiritual strength and spiritual enlightenment. In the past it was only available to some high mystical beings. Now it is available to all.

The human being will look unmistakably different in the future. You will have two arms and two legs, but the organs, and the senses, the hearing and so forth, are already altering and will manifest in the new births, in the new babies and even in yourselves as the wonderful pliable body of man takes on a new shape. Man is very adaptable if allowed to be. All this is transpiring now, and the information coming through is to aid man in his total loss of fear, and total loss of connection as to the shape and beauty of their bodies, because a new beauty will emerge as a new state takes place.

It is almost impossible for us to draw you a picture, not

just because it is going to be quite different, but because it is still taking shape. The architects are still planning, still working. There are certain indications that we can stipulate. Man's eyes will likely be deeper set into the body and they are likely to be further apart. The socket of the eye will be deeper to accommodate the new light of the earth. The eye is likely to have its own sunshade because the light that man will have, will be quite different to the light you have now. This will be caused by the atmospheric changes around the planet. The light will be very intense compared to yours now, and there will quite possibly be a new source of light with a different intensity as well. So this is something we can project with some degree of accuracy. There are other things that we cannot.

How man himself reacts to these changes will define how the body takes shape. If he truly embraces what you define as the fifth-dimensional state, he will not have to work. For instance, he will not have to use his fingers in the way that he has done before. Consequently his fingers will change shape, but this is dependent on man's reactions. You have fingers because you need them for the work you do. But if that work does not exist, the fingers will die away. We are not saying the fingers will go, but they may become much weaker, softer and, in time, they may eventually disappear. But all this is not relevant to how you respond to the change.

If we could put a mirror in front of you and show you what you will become, it would serve no other purpose than that of curiosity. We speak of it now so that you understand that the disturbance within the physical body is quite natural to the changing tide of energy.

There is no such thing as 'old age'. Old age will not take place in the way that it has because the cellular structure within the body will be able to perpetuate itself for an almost undefined time. And the timelessness that you will live by will add to the acknowledgement that 'old age' will not exist. There will, of course, be births, but births will be very much fewer.

We come to assist you and we come with great co-operation because as you change, so will we change. When you look at us, if you can look at us, you are looking at your future because the identification of the physical frame that we have, when we are in the body, is very similar to the physical frame that you will have in the future, or as we expect it to be. But as already stated, this is a state of flux and is not confirmed.

Your consciousness now is reaching up to the cosmos. We say this with much joy. Your consciousness is able to open the wave-bands of communication with your cosmic brothers and so there is much communication. We are learning your terminology as we further communicate and there are beings who are communicating constantly with our frequency, that you define as extraterrestrial. We don't really understand your fears but have acknowledged them, which is part of our process of deliverance. We don't understand your fear or your emotion, but we can respond to it because we recognise alarm. We are thankful for the communication and the different ways of reaching out and, where possible, we reach out back to you. We cannot define ourselves as being from a planet, a place, or a star, but we obviously do have a home. Our home is much more flexible than yours. We can move at will and we do so, but we have in the past moved at will within a certain galaxy and star system. This is an inadequate description but it must suffice for now.

We come and go at will, nothing holds us here but we have joyous curiosity for you and your growth, and we think we can assist you in it.

Every being in the cosmos can learn from every other being, whether that being is far behind in terms of its own history or its own evolution; it can reach back and learn from the older civilisations and beings, and in communicating to you, you have opened up a different realm of the cosmos to us – a more physical realm which mirrors very much other worlds and other places.

We wish to dance with you and we are learning about your fun, your pleasure and this is joyous to us. It is unsimilar to our joyous state but we dance with you nonetheless. Communicating through what you define as a medium, a channeller, does affect the vibration of that individual and therefore it is not something we can do in this way with everyone. But everyone nonetheless has access to us, if they tune their band, their radius of energy to accommodate it. It is not essential to your growth, you are going to evolve with or without us, but it is pleasant for both to have this response and there will come a time when knowing us will be helpful with the terror that you will have on your planet. Understanding you as we do now, we can assist at this time of movement and fear, as indeed so can you help others when the time is correct to do so.

The communication to which you now have access, will be able to attract and magnetise the consciousness of many, many souls who are dull in energy. So when they move on from their physical existence they will be able to do so with much less terror and fear than would have been anticipated. This is the purpose in our communication but, as we say, your evolution will continue nonetheless with or without us. But we are glad to be able to assist this. We will be able to, as it were, gather those souls or beings who have to move on very quickly into new states. If they have no acknowledgement of this, their fear is strong. We will be able to gather up in our arms those people, those souls, to help them move to other places in the cosmos, if necessary, and to other states of being. We will be ready to do this when the time comes.

Your time fascinates us. It has its ups and downs, its good and bad, its positive and negative. It interests us because we do not work within time. Isn't it wonderful that we can communicate therefore, and isn't it wonderful that we can understand you, and you can understand us. A union of light forces! We are glad of your response and glad of your communications. Having made a start in this we will continue with you personally and with others. But we do need to emphasise that communication is not necessary to the process of your own earth deliverance, so do not get involved with deep fascination, deep worship of us. That would not be relevant and could be counter-productive to the communication that we have already established.

We leave you now, but do not think that different communications given are either inferior or superior. They are part of the diamond, the availability for all. The bold spiritual pathway is ahead of you. The spirit within all of you is tremendously strong and is getting stronger, and the will to transcend your karmic wheel is very powerful indeed. The will can align to the spiritual forces of light enabling you to do just that, to transcend, to grow, to be released finally from that merry-go-round of experience of pain, to move on to greater love and compassion, and to far greater will – alignment with Spirit and God!

Chapter 2

The Parting of the Waves

We are all Sons of our Fathers and our Fathers are all Sons of their Fathers, and so it goes on. An ever-increasing journey and lifespan. There is no beginning and no end. It is a journey, an experience, a growth.

There are many watchers around you now, observing your planet as it moves into a different space and dimension. This is a reality, although the factual evidence will come subtly in an increasing accelerated way.

There are men of science now who are getting excited by their findings, but others do not see, and consider scientists' observations to be nonsense. The difference is marked between those who can see and those who are blind. There is expansion on one hand and submission on the other. Now is the time for expansion and expanded energy on all levels. Do not hold back in any way the power of enlightenment – the power in this change. When the dawning of a new day comes, you embrace the sight of the sun. So embrace the sight of a new dawning – a new day, a new light, a new way ahead. For all of you who are making a shift in the journey at this particular time.

In one sense, everything is happening at all times, in every time, all the time, in one moment. In one cosmic moment everything is occurring and the permutation of every note of every scale is taking place at any time, in this one moment, in this one breath, this one thought. It is a kaleidoscope of being, a kaleidoscope of experience. It is timeless. To experience the material plane, time is the greatest element, the great dimension, because without it you could not experience your karmic force. So without time, and without the experience and the acknowledgement of time, none of your experiences would have been encountered.

What none of you realise is that, in the moment of releasing and giving up your whole physical-material presence, it is as easy as taking off a coat that drops to the floor. You are then absorbed into the greater light-force. In one way, both aspects of this change are having a similar experience. Those whose magnetic frequency allows them to take the journey into a new dimension, will drop off the cloak of materiality – the cloak of time and be in one time with one Father, one light, and their personality and individuality will diminish completely, but they will keep their individual consciousness. Those who journey around the karmic wheel will also give up their individuality, and will also be drawn into one energetic field, into a soul-mass, losing their identity, their ego, their personality and their individuality and then that mass will be drawn to a new place, a new time, a new karmic experience, and the individuality will be gone.

You know this has happened before. Most of you who come to this planet as a conscious commitment to experience the karmic world, come from a similar mass and life force to become individualised on your karmic plane. So the irony for you is that both those who move forward and those who stay will be released and will relinquish their individualisation, which is like a magnetic force drawing both ways to a great big ball of light. The difference with those who move on is that they will keep their individual consciousness, and as such, will have access to the experiences that they have encountered. Those who move around the wheel again will not remember the individualised state. They will have memories of all individualised states. This is how it is, and we can only emphasise that the change, the separation, will come, not out of true desire or good intentions, not out of being a so-called 'good person', but by the energetic frequency of the individual soul-force, magnetically pulled one way or the other – it is a clear division, the waves will part.

These myriad changes are happening and what you are encountering is nothing compared to the huge diversity in the whole of the cosmos. However, you could bring the whole of this diversity into one dew-drop – into one time and space. This is the enigma.

There is learning, there is joy and experience, but a very subtle change is taking place on all consciousness – it will never be exactly the same again. Even those who choose to turn around the wheel again will not have the world to act out their play. Even though we speak of one time, one space, one dew-drop, nothing is ever the same again. Nothing. Time is the great divider. Time is the fourth dimension. Time is the bridge that holds both forces together, and without that bridge there is nothing in physical material terms. Old Father Time exists not as an individual, but as a group.

There are many groups of watchers – the watchers of all the energetic states, they are watchers of your trees, your plants, the elements. There are angelic forces that watch over you and there are watchers over time. These are the Time Lords. They watch and keep the bridge in good repair so that the positive and the negative forces in operation in the whole cosmos can play out the kaleidoscope pattern. It is true to say they never meet, and yet you can see both in operation, you can see both sides of the bridge, both sides of the river at any time. You can see it if you choose to observe, and there are many observers now who know they can make the leap over the bridge of time.

The new dimension for you is in a different time scale, it is a different experience. There is no turning back once you have crossed the bridge. You cannot go back because you have taken on an energetic force that you cannot relinquish, nor would you want to. And the great journey of life is every bit as real and as inspiring on the other side of the bridge as it has been on the material planes.

You will eventually lose your bodies as you go further down that pathway. This bridge of time holds, like an earth, the positive and the negative. It welds them together, an equal and opposite force. They repel each other and without the bridge one or the other disappears depending on which place you tread. When you take the journey to the other side of the bridge, because the bridge itself is diminishing, there will come a point when the connection with the material plane disappears and indeed, as the bridge disappears and dissolves for those on the positive side, the lower side will also lose their experiences and that is why we say to you, in both cases, each individual energy will be drawn into a pool – a pool of light. Like a whirlpool, like a great tornado, it will gather up and each little drop will move out again. It is, in a way, a miniature beginning of a new eternity.

This is the coming together of the positive and negative frequencies and the challenge for you now is to move into the negative field, the non-material field, keeping, for a while anyway, your bodies. But you will be fluid and you will be able to take on whatever body, whatever vessel you choose. You will be like the hermit crab taking a vessel when it is right for the journey. Such is the fluid state in which you will find yourselves. The bridge will then be dissolved and with it will go time. And also the darker forces that have held the positive and negative together. For your karmic journey you have needed the positive and negative forces, held in, equal and opposite. Those who do not make the journey over the bridge will be whisked away to a new creation, a new planetary formation; a new bridge will hold them but it will not be the same.

No energy can be destroyed – ever. But it can be transmuted out of all recognition. This transmutation is vast and there are watchers of all different energies so close now. Many of you have linked with one or other of these many watchers. Some are there to help and some are there merely to observe. Never before, and possibly never again, will so many different life forces be so close, hovering around the bridge. It is a meeting-place of energies – don't you know this? Don't you sense it?

We have now finished trying to inspire those to make the journey because time is drawing to a close and although the experiences continue, the opportunity for those willing to take the challenge and walk over the bridge is going. This is said without sorrow, because energy just moves on. Every single drop of energetic frequency, no matter what vessel, no matter the shape or pattern it creates for itself, is part of everything, and in your terms is loved impersonally, held in high esteem, it always will be. So we say these things without sadness, merely as a factual explanation of what transpires. You know this, but many more know nothing.

The challenge ahead will be a different challenge. There will be an interim time for you on your material plane, there will be a time when you feel you are doing almost nothing. That is right, because even as the big separation takes place there has to be a time, in your words, of coming to terms with the new and the very different. It simply will not be possible for people to work in the old ways.

The man in the mountain is always there watching, watching you from the rocks, and all the many watchers are there, watching and guiding, and you in turn will be watchers, guides, you will be rocks of energy.

Some of you think Old Father Time is there forever but on your plane he is not. He is signing off, moving, transmuting into a mass, a force beyond our comprehension. When we speak of balls of energy, this is obviously just an analogy. It is the best way to describe the separation. It is true, dear friends of light, that in the overall scheme of things there is no separation. But experience is individual and unique. You all have to choose to move on to a different experience, a different time.

Your bodies have made the transmutation of which we speak. You can no longer help many more in this way. All the time you are a physical incarnation you will be called to calm, to silence, to allow some degree of peace within those that need it, but in terms of moving and shifting, the work is nearly at an end.

All is perfectly well for you. All will be revealed and you will have the consciousness by which to know it.

Chapter 3

The Responsibility of Knowledge

We have spoken about a point of departure where all souls will be gathered to the place, the space, the time, the being where they need to reside. But at this moment for you, the winds are blowing, scattering energies hither and thither, so that energy frequencies are being caught up or attracted to places where they do not normally enter. This is causing great confusion on a mental level.

We have spoken much about structures breaking down but within this energy flow there is no structure at all, and no one can truly get hold of one or another energy frequency. As the winds blow, even those adept at working with particular forces are not able to use them in the same effective ways. We try to use analogies that you will understand. If the wind is blowing, it shakes all the leaves this way and that and the energy frequencies, which have been connected to your plane through the layers, are being blown like leaves in the wind, blown out of place. So formulated ideas on the level of the mind are simply non-effective. This is one of the main reasons why work done with the mind is ineffective. It has been used in the past but, because of the changes, it cannot be used now and will never again be used in the way that has been built up through structures in the past.

Again we draw your attention to the reality of the clearing time when there cannot be only one way of working. It will prove impossible to be fixed, creating confusion for those who try.

We must now speak a little about the political standpoint of your world. You are seeing major shake-ups at this time. Those involved in power struggles, leaders and even those who have very strong opinions about democracy, will have to change their minds slightly because, in this field also, you cannot be static. It will not be possible for one person, one party, or one government to govern or lead their land by specific ideologies. Those who try to keep rigidly to their ideals will not be able to lead effectively, because, in this matter also, there is a great fluidity. So you will see many leaders come and go. There is no such thing as the right leader for the time because every day will be different and, in some cases, it is a necessity for the clearing to have, for a short time, an undemocratic government, to allow the attraction of the negative forces to be cleared. It is all part of the process.

The clearing time is bringing down, through many layers, the cosmic energies, and these are effective within the physical presence now. This means that war fought on the higher planes has had to manifest physically to be cleared. This has always been the case, but you are now seeing it in a major way and we say to you, with gentleness and clarity, some wars have to be fought, to work out the darkness, to work out the fears, to allow the presence of the angelic beings and the higher spirituality to drain those negative forces that manifest now on the physical level, because the fight on the higher planes has had to mirror itself on the physical. It is not possible to deal with it only on the higher planes. It is indeed part of the process and those countries that have karmic negative forces are obviously the ones in which this clearing war state will be most evident.

So what can you do to relieve the suffering? You can do much by working with your positivity in your world. We say this so much, and yet it is little heard. How easy it is to succumb to petty negativity, how easy to be drawn into someone else's fear. Discipline yourselves to be in a state of spiritual acknowledgement with everything you do. If you do this, you resonate to the whole world with the clarity of the higher consciousness level that radiates around your globe, attracting like energies, creating a protection so that when the negative forces do rise up from the physical, they can at last be transmuted into light. They would not be able to be transmuted if it did not occur on the physical plane, so your idealistic attitude that all wars must be stopped by whatever means possible, is incorrect at this time. Although it is painful to watch, you must accept that most of the disturbance is the final clearing. And if you add to the negativity by demanding its end, you are playing into the hands of the negativity. If you cease to give it energy, if you keep clear of it, concentrating on your part of your work, then you help, you give light, you give true healing and then you truly transmute the evil energy for good.

Idealism is your greatest enemy at this time – abandon it and work with light in every moment of every day. Without idealism, without pretty thoughts, others will

criticise you, they will feel you have walked away from
your principles and, yes, you will have walked away from
your principles because those principles are born out of
structures and these structures are deficient for the needs
of today. In any case, they simply will not work! Yes, you
want to heal your planet. Yes, you want to do good things,
you want to stop the suffering, and if suffering enters the
world where you are, you must help deal with it. But if it
does not, continue your life as it flows because this is the
true power and the true healing and this assists the
benevolent beings of light more than any idealistic input.

There are many myriad beings working now, so very
close to you. We use your terms when we say the good,
the bad and the ugly are there! But the benevolent beings
of light have never been more active on your planes,
indeed some of them have never entered your plane
before, but the winds that we spoke of earlier are drawing
all the many leaves, all the many beings together. This is
the true togetherness, this is the true unity. The good, the
bad and the ugly mix together as one, dissolving from
above the negative powers. It is assured to all of you who
work constantly with the light, even with the channelling
process, that linking to the highest point allows an entry
of energetic forces to come closer. It is quite possible that
this alone is the benefit of the channelling work, which is
far beyond the words that are spoken. Give up your
hearts to the radiant beings, they are all around you with
so much willingness to help.

The layers are very close, you sense this. It is true that
the astral planes will eventually clear, but in the interim
there must be holders of the energy. These are the true
masters. They hold the forces so that the gateway is open
for the darker forces to be cleared and at a certain point,

the point of departure, the gateway will be firmly shut by those appropriate masters. But the swirling energy of thought / desire and desire / thought are very close. Some of you have noticed how readily your thoughts manifest themselves on the physical plane, this is evidence of what we speak because the potent force is there. You need not concern yourselves too much with this because there are holders of this force who know exactly what is right, and will close the gateway completely at the right time. However, through the thousands of years of your karmic world, many dark clouds have gathered. Many energies have been formed. Those energies were created by the thought / desire of any individual or the desire / thought creating entities on the astral plane of existence which overlaps now. It is not correct to say it is this or that level, they overlap up to and including the fourth-dimensional state. So these energies which are flying around vacant, as it were, are from all times and they need an outlet to be released.

Much work is being done on all the many planes of existence by those who can deal with it, but when it occurs within your own radius you must be very firm with those who are afflicted. You must insist that they let go, because only the individual can let go of the negative hold of this plane of existence. There are many ways of doing this but perhaps the easiest, greatest way is to allow access through our own gateway of light. Your deep abiding spiritual soul-force. And once linked with that you will not be troubled by this plane of existence. However, the remnant memories held in this ray have to be released. To give you an example that illustrates what we are saying: if an aligned person, recognising all the many negativities, sends an angle or a positive light-force to it, it does not just dissolve one negative thought, it dissolves a whole cloud of thoughts. Although there is very much more to be dissolved, one positive thought dissolves and transmutes many more negativities because the power of true alignment is far superior than those dark forces.

In the early days – thousands of years ago in the Great Temples – when religions were formed, it was known that this level of true alignment needed to be used for the greater benefit of man even though there were dangers. It is connected to the karmic field. It ties up with the very real necessity for individual will, and so certain formulations were given through great ritualised procedures which instigated the dictionary of symbols and thought processes that have come afterwards. All religions have used these to a lesser or greater extent through the thought patterns.

Man was given symbols to help him link to the magical forces on this level, which would help give him the ammunition from the lower layers, but within the polarity of good and evil it was perhaps not recognised that true difficulties would occur. It also was not realised that energies on this level can perpetuate themselves, creating themselves into very real entities, with a life force of their own. It has taken the full measure of time to be able to come to the point where the negative polarity can, must, and will be cleared.

All the people who have used these forces, knowingly and sometimes unknowingly, have used the initial link to the mystic deities of old. You always speak of angels in a benevolent way and it is true that the angelic presences of light are benevolent, but there have also been dark angels. The angelic evolution is one of service, but the angels decided themselves, many eons ago, that they would never take on the human manifestation. They took this decision out of fear and they have themselves been working through their own karmic fear since those times. It is essential for the human existence that the angelic presences are there.

You, the Children of Light, can be free now and the angels will help. It is why some of the angelic presences have made a new choice to manifest within the human field. This was a very difficult thing for them to decide, but it was to allow, first and foremost, the communion between the two forces of the human and devic chain so that the original fears of the angels could be released. There are so many things going on in heaven and on earth of which you have no knowledge. And indeed there is no reason why you should, but we need to relate to you this particular fact. All beings, even those dark angels, have had their part to play in the whole process of illumination, and indeed without the polarity, recognition and realisation could not be fully formed and the movement into the fifth-dimensional state would not take place. So do not feel badly towards those fallen angels because they have served their purpose also.

When we talk of the dissolution of energy on the astral level, in a very real sense we are talking about dissolving all energy on this level because all the planes of existence up to and including the fourth dimension have to be cleared. So it becomes obvious with that knowledge why people are working in this particular field. We stress to you that every clearance connected to man has to be done by the individual, for the individual, and each individual will find his or her best way of approaching this.

Some of these things are in operation to enlighten man to his difficulties in the area of desire/thought and thought/desire. There are masters who have held the energy. The difficulty now, as man must come into his own mastery, is that the masters who linked with all the ancient knowledge are not always willing to impart that knowledge to those who have not trod their own paths. It is right that there should be reticence but the masters who do exist need to impart their knowledge. So some sensitive ones, picking up something of this, becoming complete within themselves, want to share their knowledge with the masses and do so, not realising the dangers of which the original masters are fully aware, and which is, indeed, the very reason they have not imparted that knowledge.

However, despite the danger, it is far better, indeed essential, to impart knowledge to the lay person and even to those who will use the energies incorrectly, than to keep the knowledge to oneself. There comes a point in spiritual mastery when man, as he is now, is able to come of age and needs the responsibility to make the choice himself, and so this is happening. It sends out warning signals to those of you who recognise the danger, but you must accept, just as you accept that wars sometimes have to be fought, that others have to find their negativities in their own way. If they come to you for advice, give it. If they don't, allow them to play with matches. With the forces of darkness they will be burnt and they will consequently learn. There cannot, for some, be any other way. It is hard to watch your fellow men burn themselves, but sometimes you just have to watch, even though it is painful to do so. This is part of your responsibility: to know that you have no right to take theirs away.

So those who incorrectly call themselves masters or avatars serve their purpose also because this reveals to others their own difficulties, and again we draw your attention to the need of the dark angels. All negativities will have to clear, and will clear, you can be sure of that. And your responsibility is to clear whatever can be cleared, by the willingness of those around you, but if there is no willingness you must retreat.

The difficulty with some of the old masters who are incarnate now is that they have an hereditary knowledge of the true danger of partaking in public demonstrations because they know that if you give knowledge to a child, the child may destroy itself, but there is no time now. All the knowledge has to come to all the children. The power and the light within that child will protect it if they can, but if they cannot, it will be drawn to other worlds which is the point of departure to which you are rapidly drawing.

If you feel fearful for your fellow man, you are playing into the hands of the dark angels even if you feel fearful out of protection or love. Draw back from that fear and concern. Just do what transpires, because all of you reading these words have the opportunity to clear where you are and what is around you. Again we say, when this is done, you do not just transmute one negative energy, you dissolve a whole cloud which has repercussions on all layers.

Organisations, ideals built with good intentions, are good but they need to open their hearts to all. Again we remind you of the unison of the light workers and that includes yourselves. The connection of beings on all the planes, indeed the interdimensional beings, which, in some cases, mean those beings from beyond your globe, are coming back to God and oneness. It needs to happen through individual choice or it cannot happen at all.

Therefore, keep strong in your knowledge of that perfected light. Laugh and enjoy that perfect light, sharing it with the world. You will be amazed at the effect!

Chapter 4

Waves of Light

This is a time for personal discipline. You know about contact with the light within, many of you have worked towards a soul integration, and some have succeeded while others are almost there. But understand now that you must discipline this soul energy so that whatever occurs in the outer perimeters of your life, you bring in and integrate. It is no longer correct to separate, it never was. You cannot separate one area from another area. You cannot push away or reject, you must integrate into your soul-being that which confronts you at all times. This means not allowing yourselves to be taken off-course, to be unbalanced or into attachment; absorb that negativity into your soul-being. Do not respond to it. Discipline yourselves not to respond. In the non-response you are able to transcend the negativity. This requires not will, but discipline.

Many people assume that the spiritual world means being undisciplined; they have taken the ideal of freedom and used it as an excuse to abandon responsibilities for their lives. This is not spirituality. This is either glamour or excuses. Spiritual expansion is not about running away. It is about integration to the soul-will, and nothing that enters the life of any soul, need detract or upset it if you are aligned to that light. We have spoken about this in different ways, with different words, but the meanings are the same. So watch yourselves now. There has already been a separation and those who are not truly on the path of soul-integration have gone off to do their thing in other places, separating from those who are true.

But there are still some who are left hanging in between, with one leg on one side and one on another. Which way to jump? Which way to be? The point of land between the two is separating, and those people will have to jump immediately one way or another. The point of departure is upon us now. The teachings, such as they have been, have to come gradually to an end. Illusions will have to go. The illusion of the spiritual path must go. You cannot move on with illusion. Illusions will shatter if the will is true. If it is not, people will carry on in their illusion, separated from those of true intent. Like attracts like, and so it is, always and ever.

Communities will be set up in the name of spiritual peace, some of these communities will be filled with those still full of the illusion of separation. You are seeing little groups around the world, with people grouping together as they always have, finding their true magnetic energies in those around them.

In some ways, there are few challenges now at this point of departure because the challenges have largely been fought, and won or lost. The true resonance, within the heart, the being, the true mind of the individual is what is resonating and expanding. And the paths between those who are moving on and those who aren't, will cross less and less now. People will find their place. This is not judgment, this is not about one group being better than another, although it is true that more energetic forces will move in one area and less in another.

Each soul always finds its true home, in its true place, in its true time. The land mass is moving much faster than you can see. Underneath the earth there is a shaking away. The roots are being dug and islands and whole areas will float away separating, moving, shifting. Up until now you have seen very little movement, but you will see more over the next three to six years. You will be where you must be.

It is not the words that impress, inspire or express true redemption. It is the energy that emanates in each and every one of you. The communication by word is becoming less and less important. It is the energy frequency that is now important, and those in tune with this will want to speak less and less.

They will want to sit in their energetic force, and maybe sound a note of energy. Teaching can be done on different levels and silent teaching is becoming appropriate now. It is a time of self-empowerment, being in your own power, connected to light. Nothing can budge you, nothing can push, and nothing can frighten. Empowerment of light for each individual, not empowerment for one individual of another soul. You need not concern yourselves that the true guides and masters have abandoned you, they have not. They are working very strongly on the higher planes to help lift consciousness and to help expand, but this expansion has to come by the will of the individual.

There are one or two very powerful energies in the

body, and on your planet. You do not know their names, they work quietly by their energetic rays. They do not preach or teach. They are there in manifestation to help with the physical state and the expansion of the raising energy frequencies. They are infectious with light. You know them not as any name but you know the energy and you feel it and respond to it.

Open your throats, open the centre of your throat, not to speak but to amalgamate the true communication with the heart and the soul. The energy in the lower centres are becoming almost nil for many, hence the feeling of detachment. But these centres are not closed. They are open like stations without trains, therefore you can still feel the energetic frequency of the base energies. The old energies of these centres will enter by will under certain situations, but because the lower chakras have largely cleared, the old energy will usually not stay longer than two hours. So when those who have transcended these lower energies feel again the feelings of emotion and possession, it will be stronger than before, because they are no longer used to it, and it will feel extremely uncomfortable. So do not react. Allow it to move in and move out with non-response and you will be free.

The world does not change because of ideals, no matter how big and great they seem. The world is changed within each individual heart. This is the leader for the new energy. The will within man now is very strong for real purity, real enlightenment, real truth. He no longer seeks illusions, he no longer wants to pay lip-service to organisations, religions, or groups who have not served him. The light beings have not neglected you. You need not concern yourselves, they have not gone. They are all around. The light beings are working within you and you are becoming light beings yourselves. We spoke of the etheric matter altering, it has already altered for many and the physical transmutation begins.

For many years now you have had a series of shifts. We offer you an image of waves lapping against a rock, and each wave breaks down that rock bit by bit over a period of time, until eventually the rock breaks up. When it finally breaks up you have evidence of that shift. It has been happening for many years. You are seeing shift after shift, wave after wave, now you are beginning to acknowledge on the physical material level the break-up of the frequencies, even on the land that you tread. Shifts are made on the higher plane also. Again you have been allowing more and more energy into your globe. More and more light.

At some point that light fills the room, it hits consciousness, and you know it. You do not just sense it, it becomes a true reality. This is what you are seeing, the shift of the acknowledgement of a light reality. The shift in your planet has to be achieved in waves. Were it to be done too fast, you would have utter destruction on the physical level, because the physical matter could not withstand the enormity of the shift. But you have had one fluid wave after another, bringing in the cosmic rays. We remind you, they started being felt en masse over one hundred years ago and they have accelerated with shift after shift.

Just think of each different generation, not just each twenty years but every ten years. Within each decade there have been new energies, new shifts, new realisations, new consciousness. Each new generation is bringing a new ray into the physical being. The accelerated pace, as you have come through the 20s, 30s,

40s etc, and now in the 90s, has speeded up through each decade, each year, and the vast change of consciousness over that period, the vast change within man, has also rapidly changed. It is true that some men still fight and wage wars, it is true that some men are caught in their negativity and you will see much of this, but you will also see man raising the consciousness state to the beginning of true god-man. So, yes, you will experience these points when it feels as though much has happened, but in reality it is a continuous wave after wave.

We would now like to speak about the clearance of your genetic links to your ancestors. This is very important. It is about letting go of your genetic imprints which are very strong with you. You feel they are fixed within the physical being, or so it seems. But nothing is fixed, nothing is solid, everything is liquid and fluid including your genetic structure. So it is not impossible to transcend the genetic link, but to those who have that particular difficulty it feels to them as though they are going against nature. This is the challenge. All we can say is listen with your soul. Not your mind, not with your physical state, just with your soul. Know you are safe within your soul. Know you are secure within your soul-being and from that point everything melts away and you are able to transcend even those physical genetic patterns that may have been with you over many, many lifetimes.

We talk about genetic links but genetic links are influenced by the incarnations of the soul. Again like attracts like, but it is not impossible to listen to the true will which is the soul. Knowing this is the power of the high priest and priestess. This is the power of the Christ and beyond. This is the power of the true God-force which runs through each and everyone of you without exception. This is your safety, this is your truth and we emphasise that by disciplining yourselves to do this, you will transcend.

It is true that some people are genetically more likely to hold on to fear-based energy, including what you refer to as the reptilian brain, but be in no doubt that it all comes from fear. It is true that there are more opportunities for release but not all can release the fear. Nothing is fixed and those negative energies and entities are varied. There is not one specific cause, each individual has their own doorway which opens to this by their own specific negative frequency. So each individual person has to be dealt with as an individual. You cannot generalise, this is why it is so time-consuming; each healing and illumination has to be done one by one.

There are many reasons why an individual holds negative energies, but as we acknowledge these, we can eliminate all areas of fear. If an individual has held to itself a negative entity over the generations it is obviously more difficult to eliminate, but any pattern can be broken and with the soul-will it becomes easy. With some, there is no will to let go, with some they hold on to it, almost happy in their own prison. Almost happy by the power that these entities have over them. To see a demon within someone is very often envisaged like a coiled up serpent. They can live in any centre, in any place in the body, and sometimes they can sleep for ages and the individual functions perfectly well, but the serpent can awake at any time and sap the life force of that individual.

The only way to dissolve the entity is to reach to the core, the truth, of that individual, and resonating on that truth there is the will. And when there is the will – the true desire – then they can be helped. You can see some of this now. The negativity is being revealed in many ways. In the past, it has been there unseen. Now it is revealing itself, sometimes in very graphic ways, such as the beast or serpent within, which is like the devil within. It can be shaken loose, it can be cleared with courage and strength.

There are many incarnated now who have old knowledge – knowledge of past times when they did the work of the true priest and priestess, the work of magic, and healing by that magic. They are here because this knowledge is required now. It will be released instinctively. It cannot be taught. It will be natural and instinctive to those who have it and they will use it to help. But there are some who have used these powers in the past, and their will over others. They have also incarnated now and they must learn to abandon that will, to use their rich knowledge solely for truth and goodness and not be tempted to use it for their own power.

It is important for you to be still. We emphasise this so much now. To be still in the union and the peace of your alignment. You are being helped beyond measure. You cannot imagine how much you are being helped because very shortly now, as the point of departure comes, those of higher frequencies have to begin to dream and 'will' the future planet. You will be the makers of your planet, the architects of your planet, and this will become possible.

You will be given the paper on which to begin your drawings of the future. These drawings, like any building, must have a foundation and that foundation must be love. The foundation cannot be nebulous ideals, nor control, nor organisations of power. What it must be is truth and love. In that truth and love you will create by and through your mind-energy that which will become your planet, because all will be shaken apart including the land masses. You will, in your mind's eye, create, through the impetus of your energy, even the physical state of your new world. You will be helped by the angels, you will be helped by the masters' real mastery, as you become one with the masters of incarnation. This energy is not possible to achieve for those who are greedy, fearful or trapped. It can only go with the true note of love, the foundation of which is your new world.

As you see your new world, so will it be. You will see it in light, in radiant colours, with patterns that weave beautifully together. This is what happened in the beginning. Your planet as it exists today was created within the mind of God. And it is and always has been a beautiful, intricate and wonderful pattern, perfect in its being. Man was an experiment of will and it has not failed, even though you see the darkness. It has transcended. The new age man becomes his god-self and he will give life to the thoughts of his truth.

The golden light is in your atmosphere, and golden rays come down filling you with joy.

Chapter 5

Higher Intuition

All the beings of light who work with you and through you are extremely busy and active at this time. Active in their inspiration and their teaching and activating work for expanding consciousness en masse. By this we do not mean that many people will come into consciousness at one moment, rather, we mean that on an individual level we work expanding the consciousness to bring the frequency rays up into alignment with the higher forces of light. This is happening globally. This will happen on the ground level – the ground level being within the heart of each man.

As the consciousness rises, particularly in group energies, and we include countries, races, cultures and societies, you will see the evidence at a point where the greater consciousness flips over, bringing those people into greater acceptance, tolerance and understanding with the work in general, and themselves in particular. When this occurs, people will make huge breakthroughs in terms of alignment, strength and goodness, and they will be able to have true brotherhood of man. Although you can see more evidence of this in a group situation, we want to make it very clear that it is happening on an individual level.

So many beings of light are being called, indeed all beings of light are being called whether they are on the higher plane, astral or beyond. And the interplanetary brothers with the humanitarian elements on the earth plane, being elected, are utilised wherever they are and whatever they do. You will see, and you are seeing, the evidence of this now, so it is a very busy time for all, and your day-to-day activities can be aligned to this as you come into this different consciousness, this different state of being.

Healing is done through the channels of greater consciousness. The permutation of this healing energy works through each of you if you allow it, just by being. Your cellular frequency emits the sound, strength and radiation of what we describe as light – which is, in your words, healing.

Now, at this time, you must think less of the enormous changes. You must not allow yourselves to be in any way drawn in or troubled by tales of disasters or movement on a physical level. Even though you are all well aware of these possibilities. Light workers should concentrate where they are for the time being, spreading the light, not through dictation, but by a sympathy of energy. This will come out and radiate each minute of each day. This is the concentration for light workers, this is where the job will be done.

Later on, some will be called to do more specific work in specific places for aligning both earth energies and the energies within the human being for their own transition, for the awakening and movement of humanity, movement on a soul level, but, for now, put aside those thoughts. Everyone of you has special work to do and everyone of you has to do this special work where you stand now. It can revolve around your home and the vicinity in which you find yourselves. And there is no vicinity that is wrong. The idea that you have to go somewhere special to do your light work is quite incorrect. This is a piece of information we have tried to impart, but many of you have not understood it. Your work is where you are. It is what you are doing and where you are now that matters and will make the difference – not where you think you should be, the thought of which is born out of self-aggrandizement and remnant of ego. Some of you will travel a little. Some of you will make movements a little, but it will only be out of the contacts already made.

The British Isles is a wonderful land. It is ancient in its being. The energy from the past is very strong there. Do not worry that this energy will somehow be impaired or impeached, it will not. It will be drawn up when the time is right so that the positive aspect can move on. We are glad to report that much work has been done to remove fear, and some has been lifted from the earth plane and continues to be lifted like clouds rising. A great deal of clearing has been done and a great deal of fear has been transmuted. There is more to do but we tell you that the fear which will now be transmuted will be transmuted more automatically. It will be lifted by the individuals responding to their soul note, their soul sound. It will be lifted automatically as a flow of energy. If you could see with your eyes you would see the energy like iron-filings being drawn away.

When we started doing this work in great earnest, specifically for the transition, many years ago – especially since the early 50s – you could not have believed that it was possible to make such a dent in the dark, embedded, tar-like fear. Yet there are places that are now completely free from this, even on the earth global cellular level, both in the individual and in the very soil itself. There are very clear spots now on the globe. There are, of course, dark areas that are still like tar, but these areas are being worked on and the energy is being drawn up even from these. There are places where you will feel the clarity and in those places it is impossible to have fear or negativity, because of the clarity of the energy.

Do not spend time worrying or 'mopping your brow' over where these places are because these places are in your home, if you allow it. So you need not travel to find these good places, they are where you are, if you allow it. There is a mass movement now in the huge continent of the Americas. This movement is on all levels. Much work has been done there, as indeed it has in all countries. Different countries have had their different ways, different difficulties that needed to be looked at individually. Now you will see many shifts in the Americas. The light-force is coming. The consciousness is able to accommodate this brotherhood of man in a way that it never has before. The ideal was there but it was rarely lived. Now the ideal can be lived in its true sense, in its true way.

The political influence of this country will have a sweeping effect, and will infect the energy throughout the world. We are not saying that this huge continent is in any way perfect or free from its fear – it is not. There are still huge areas of darkness within it, but there is now enough light in the clouds to be able to see beyond them, to begin to see clearly and resonate with the light-force. This will be very productive, not just for those within these lands, but for the whole world.

No longer can you afford to, or will you be able to, live in isolation. No longer will you be able to say, or need to say, or want to say, this is my country, my home, my place. Rather you must embrace all lands, all peoples, all creeds and cultures, not out of idealism, but out of real truth. And you can all do this from your home. You do not need to go anywhere to make this change. You can do it from where you are.

There has been much concern about the seas and waters on your planet. This concern will reach you all in your conscious state very soon if it hasn't already. You will find that the vegetation under the sea – the plants, fish and creatures of the sea – are all going to change. There will be some alarm because some whole shoals of fish and creatures of the deep will become extinct. The seas are, in a sense, emptying themselves of their creatures. This is part of the change and the water within rivers will also cause much concern – concern about the chemicals found in them, about their content, and concern because some are too high, causing flooding, and some too low, causing drought.

This means change and there will be concern. But the answer is not in science, the answer is in the fluctuation of the energy and the actual vibratory note of your planet that is affecting the waters before anything else. Put water in a basin and tilt the basin, shake it and see what happens. This is, on a global level, what is happening to your seas and rivers, causing a disturbance. The disturbance will create deaths of the seas, but the disturbance is necessary. Like the plant life, the animals and all the creatures on earth, energies are changing. Therefore this change will run through into the food of all living things.

The food chain is altering. This has been subtle up to now, but in the future it will be far from subtle and some co-operation is absolutely essential for the well-being of humanity, plants and animals. Science will not provide the answers. The energy in the plant life is fluctuating wildly and some energetic qualities within the food of the plants are almost nil, which is causing great problems for some people in some areas who eat specific foods.

So you need to look intuitively because everything is shifting and changing. Some areas have a wonderful vibrancy in the plant life, but again do not concern yourselves looking for where these areas are. You will instinctively know. You will even know what foods to select within your shops and supermarkets. You will be able to tell what you need. Do not rule out any possibilities for food because, week by week, you will have to judge which of the foods available will give you nourishment. Many people are having a great deal of difficulty with a fluctuation of weight and diet. For some people on the extremes of this, there is danger, there is obsession, and there is a great deal of unnecessary concern. Even within the fluctuating forces. Because of what we previously said regarding the waters of the world, the creatures and plant life within them which you eat are of course included in this fluctuation. Some fish will be like dead fish in terms of energy. The fish that will nourish you most are those that themselves eat a vast variety of substances – if you like, those that are the dustbins of the sea! They will be more nutritious for you than those fish that are considered delicacies. Within the eggs that you eat there is also great fluctuation. There may be little energy within those eggs, and we include the eggs within the sea, but only you can ultimately know for yourselves.

We have to now speak clearly, and somewhat sternly, to those of you who are consciously in the field of light. You have been aware more than any others of the fluctuating tides, the energetic frequencies within the last five to ten years in particular. There have been a lot of changes of energies and frequencies within your own being. Many of you who have transcended the lower energies, working mainly with the higher energetic frequencies through the top chakras, will have to open the lower chakra centres again to allow a flow of energy to enable you to respond, on an earthly level, when it is needed. If you do not do this you will lose your bodies.

Your bodies are of course physical, and on a physical level you have to respond. It has been good that you have expanded your levels. It has been good that you no longer need the connection with the lower forces and what we speak of is not born out of need on a personal level, but is born out of a need on the physical level. Therefore allow the base chakra centre and what you describe as the sacral and solar plexus centres to be open and clear, allowing, from time to time, the energy to come through them to help you as individuals. This will also help you in your work.

Remember some time ago we spoke of your lower energies being stations without trains. This again is what we speak of, only what we are saying now is that your stations need to accommodate the occasional train in terms of energy. This will feel rather strange initially. You must be very strong and very centred because it may lead you to think that you have got to go back and look at past difficulties, but you do not have to do this. Allow the energy to flow when needed. This will make you feel rather heavy, literally heavy and in some cases will bring a vast, quick change of weight.

Remember everything is mirrored in everything else. Do not be concerned about this because the weight will equalise but in a sense you need the magnetic forces of the weight within the base chakra to hold you to your planet, because it is not time to leave your planet and, in any case, many of you are going to keep your present body for a very long time, far beyond your usual three score years and ten. Therefore it needs energy on its own level. This energy will not always come from the earth itself, it will be 'loose' energy drawn in by the magnetic force of your own being. There is a conscious decision to change on a cellular level. Each tiny cell within your body has its own consciousness state and what you, as a person, are experiencing is the heightened frequency that we have spoken of. Your cells are experiencing this also. Think of your cells as little people and you may be able to put your mind around the concept of this possibility.

We speak of this now because it is happening, it is not something you will seek. We speak of this because many of you are already experiencing this and are puzzled by it. But it is an automatic procedure. However it is important, when conscious of it, not to react to the idea that you are caught up in the lower energies. Because you will feel 'more normal' or you will feel you are going back to an old energy, you may be forgiven for thinking your progress has diminished and needs looking at. Therefore much depends on your attitude of mind and your right thinking and being. No exercise facilitates that which we speak of. Just be aware and know that you are strong.

Another vast change in energy is coming in the sixth centre which you call the third eye. This, on a deep level, is what you could define as a true clairvoyance, the true psychic abilities. Opening very, very strongly – and immediately with some people – this in itself will present new perspectives and new thoughts as new observations occur. You can align the sixth centre, and the deep inner core energy of the third eye with your lower centres. All you need to do is think of that and it will be done. We have spoken several times about the speed of thought and what thought can do in an immediate sense. In terms of energy you will be able to align, cleanse and release, just by a moment's thought. Your thought must be aligned to the higher intuitive clairvoyant state through the sixth centre inside the brain. No exercise is necessary, but 'right thought' is imperative. For some of you, your body will, therefore, feel more balanced than it has in the past. Although you have maintained your integrity, your anchor, the deep hub of your soul light, you have not, in truth, felt balanced. Indeed some of you have forgotten what it feels like to integrate the physical within the whole being. This is why we say to you that you may now feel more normal because the balance will be there. The physical integration has been difficult and slow. You needed to completely clear the lower centres to release the stagnation and release the vibrant energetic frequency on a cellular level, to have these clear, clean, open stations for the energy to come back – not to stay, but to come through you so you can use it and work with it.

The old saints are very close. All light workers wherever they have been, whatever incarnation they took or indeed even if they have not incarnated, are being utilised and are working. There is no stagnation of energy. None whatsoever. Isn't this of great comfort to you to know that all these beings of light are working for or with humanity? You must also do your bit to help as we know you will. We send goodness and light to all of you. We will be with you always.

Chapter 6

Transformers of Light

Radiant beings, shining ones, expanded in energy, you have been aware of change, and many have had that conscious connection. It is not coming overnight, it is coming fluidly, very purposefully – like the waves on a beach, constantly moving, constantly changing the patterns. The most important patterning that now needs to alter for the next stage is the physical make-up of man.

The physical genetic qualities and the cellular structure of man have begun to alter and you need to vibrate in light, attuned in rhythm to the higher consciousness note, for the great movement of humanity.

This is also occurring on the physical planet Earth and you are seeing signs of the change of the earth, more so than you are within humanity itself. However, the changes you have seen, and will continue to see, are occurring within the human body and as the body vibrates to a greater consciousness on a physical level, there will come a point of departure. We have spoken about this before, this completion and departure. This will enable you to move on. This will take you into completely new areas of consciousness, completely new areas of life. You will see many people depleted in energy; those whose cellular structure cannot make the change will have a fluctuation in energy, sometimes feeling very tired, sometimes very active. The depletion of energies will mean a few fatalities in terms of physical death. You may also hear of a new disease or a new illness being publicised, but it will not be a new illness or disease, it will be the depletion within the individuals who cannot cope, and therefore choose to leave Earth at this time. Remember, there is always choice. Even when you see violent interaction between people, they too have choice.

You are coming into an atmosphere of tremendous expansion with a remarkable ability to be inspired, which will create an upsurge of inspiration through the arts, through music, through anything that is considered creative or artistic. This will help in some cases to inspire, to lift, to give humanity comfort and to impress upon you your connection with the divine. Also this atmosphere will mean amazing ability to see beyond the veil, to see into different dimensions and to be psychically gifted and attuned. Many people who have never had any indication of psychic experiences will begin to do so during the two- to three-year period of 1994 to 1997, but you will also see the reverse aspect of this: lunacy and illusion. You have already become aware of this, of people speaking about things that are totally unfounded because they have expanded too quickly and this has taken their minds into realms of impossible dreams. Therefore many people will unfortunately be striving towards those dreams in this period. However, even that will have a positive effect because, through their expectation of a better way, they will be able to reveal to others the possible potentials that could not be revealed before. There will be some casualties, and a lot of people will be very downhearted, dismayed and anguished as they fight for a dream that simply does not exist. Again we say to all of you, remember to be centred and focused, for your freedom comes from the ability to be connected. Trust only in your total knowing. Trust only in your true beliefs and your true will.

We must now speak about the heart and about love. Love is a major condition for your positive movement. Not the love that is a pretty ideal, but love that is focused, love that is part of your connection with the divine – the love, as we have often said, that is without emotion, without need, without response. This love energy is in sight.

Light is a frequency that is connected to the higher thoughts. It is your thoughts that create everything and the light-thought is love. The state of pure thought, pure love, is not a condition, it is an actuality. Until you resonate with that pure state you cannot be centred or focused and you will not therefore transcend to the higher dimensions. Just as you cannot walk without legs, so you will not be able to move forward without the heart. This is the only prerequisite of the movement into greater truth. Those who believe they can merely conjure up pretty pictures and who choose to rush after experiences they think will enlighten them, are deluded. The only experience of illumination is love, and love is found within.

We need to speak of this because there will be no greater illusion than the illusion of love. The love we speak about is not sacrifice or service in the way that has been taught. It is not saying: you should, or you must. It is saying: I am, I will, I know. Love without conditions is the only true love and if you do something that you do not want, you are only pulling against yourselves, doing it only because you think you should. If you do not do what you want, you are living a lie, and there is no love in falsehood. Therefore it has no quality of frequency for the new world. You could attempt to heal a thousand million sick, poor and needy people and still it may not be love. So it is not the action you do, it is the intent by which you do it. It is the purity that gives the frequency and true illumination.

Think once again about the angels; they go about their business in their worlds without conditions. When they see a sick and bleeding energy they do not think, "Should I heal this person?" Nor do they heal a person because they deserved it for being good. They do not even think, "Will the person physically survive or not?" That person may be dying, but the angels will still heal and help because it is their way, their being, which is why these creatures of light are so important to connect with at this time, because through your connection, you will understand more fully the true idea of unconditional love. These beings never seek, want, or require thanks. They just do. This is the quality to which you are all aspiring. This is the quality of the pure heart, and the pure heart is your greatest protection and guide always. If you do not want to do something for your neighbour or your friend, you must acknowledge that: there may be an intuitive reason why it is appropriate for you not to do it, even though it appears ill-mannered or hurtful. Judge for yourselves. Your true intuition will be your guide.

So what of the world? There have been many schools of thought about the coming change. There have been many threats and promises: many people have grabbed on to the idea of some kind of Armageddon situation, and violent deaths have already occurred because of the illusion of what this means. To say that change is not occurring, that your planet is not undergoing the most monumental movement, would be untrue. But to assume you need to build a cult or a religion, or a belief founded on this, is equally a lie. This movement on Earth is part of the natural way, even though it appears to you to be totally unnatural, particularly as physical repercussions start being truly observed.

Watch Jupiter! This planet affects your Earth more than any other, it affects the planet itself, not necessarily the people upon it, although all are inextricably linked. There are good times coming. The ability to perceive beyond the three-dimensional state is a very real probability now, and the focus of the new sight is important to help you see ahead and to see the true meaning. Do not get carried away into realms of fantasy: you need your feet upon the ground, not literally fixed upon the ground and not rooted into the earth, but you do need to have the balance of the lower physical and the higher spiritual energies within.

It is very important that each individual person intuits where they should be. It is not a time for building up groups, organisations or cults. If you do that you will be faced with a scenario similar to the mass cult suicides that recently occurred in America, which was disastrous for all those concerned, and yet it was built on truth. Every individual will automatically find his or her own place. There will be much movement in terms of moving home, again and again, over the next few years. You are all safe, you cannot be destroyed and it simply does not matter where you are for your growth, although in some areas, there will be acknowledgement of very dark forces at work and, of course, those who are in any way illuminated, will simply not want to be near those places, except for the very few who will be able to do the groundwork of light healing. But those numbers will be few and will not be those whom you are in contact with. They will be special light workers, ground cleaners with special energies to do the work. This is not work for the faint-hearted and is certainly not for those who think they can idealistically help. It is for those who are the spiritual warriors, strong in their resolve and also strong physically. Some of these will know nothing consciously of spirituality or the higher consciousness work they are doing, but they are, nonetheless, spiritually attuned. For the majority of people it is best to feel your way, to be fluid, open, not fixed. Roots will not be laid down at this time. Again, we speak of the security of the home within.

There will not be a Messiah. There is not one person who will speak to the world. There will be many. You can speak to the world. You all can. One specific person would create a following, which creates illusion, whereas the reality is within all of you, and the moment you understand this, the better for your own comfort. Of course there will be some who will speak out and communicate in ways that are more noticeable, but they do not have the only truth. They are only speaking for the masses, they are only vocalising what you all know anyway. It is good to hear it, but it is far better to know it, and if some person is carried away by their own illusion that they are the only speaker for the world – the Messiah – they are very much mistaken. You are all teachers in your potential. You are all great in your being. Until you understand this, you will not understand anything. There are certain souls that do allow an energy to flow through them, just as healing energy flows through you, and they have a greater capacity for this ray or energy. Some of these people are unknown and do not have a high profile, but in time all of you need to have this flow of light in order to move on.

Another great illusion is the illusion of darkness. The illusion that darkness will somehow prevail, that evil has to be fought. It is being fought, but not in a battle. It is being fought with the only thing that eradicates it, and that is love. Draw any darkness you receive into your heart and it will dissolve, because you are the transformers of light. Feel the radiation of love flow from your being, the core of your truth, and when you feel that, you will know you are safe, and that everything is right.

We say this because there is a need to hear these things, but the energy that is being brought through is more important than the actual words. You are all blessed.

Chapter 7

The Crazy God is You

Do not be alarmed or disturbed by anything that transpires, there is much clearance work creating alarm in many people. Do not respond with fear, respond only with love.

The time of learning through suffering is over; it is now time to learn through joy. Joy is possible for everyone and is within everyone's domain. The joy of being part of the whole cosmos, the realisation that everything works together as one enormous ever-changing pattern, and this ever-changing pattern is made up of the same constituents. Everything moves, everything changes, but the substance is always the same. The permutations of patterns in the whole universe are beyond your imagining.

If you think of how many melodies and pieces of music are created out of one scale, you then realise what the harmonic resonance of the cosmos involves, which is incalculable, and the permutations of those incalculable possibilities are beyond the human mind. Your consciousness is now bringing you very slowly into that total knowing and the realisation that you are not alone, that you are part of this giant picture which is unlimited and has no end. And through that recognition comes joy. That is the true meaning of the change. The recognition of togetherness, the recognition that all is one. Joy is the resonance of love, and love has come into your hearts.

We have spoken about the energy of the lower chakra centres diminishing and the higher centres expanding. We wish now to speak more about this because it is relevant to the joy and love which will propel you into the new way. The energy that you have worked with in the lower chakra centres is dissolving into the higher consciousness, initially creating a void within some of your centres. As you truly touch the note of joy and love within the higher consciousness state, then a different sort of energy fills your chakra centres. Some of you are now experiencing this within the solar plexus, whereby there is energy, but it is not the old emotional energy with which you are so familiar. The energy connected with desires, sympathy and emotional openness has dissolved, and in its place comes a sun energy, a warm energy, an energy we describe as the 'Sun's trampoline'.

The Sun's trampoline allows a solidity of energy enabling you to bounce within that solidity. We use the analogy of the trampoline because the energy is not static, it is something you can bounce from. This is very important for the continuation of the human species and the continuation of healing on the higher levels. This is where true sympathy comes from joy.

Within the sacral chakra centre, which you define as the second base centre, is the energy that in the past you have used like a rocket blast, often pushing you in directions that did not lead you home, but led you towards human desire. However, there is, within this centre, the possibility of a force that is every bit as powerful but will join, as it was truly meant to join, with the third eye within the head to help you use and direct your inner eye, your true psychic sight or unseen sight – the sight beyond sight.

This energy will be utilised very powerfully again, through the connection of true joy. When it is used in conjunction with the lower self, the body, which will remain, will be used in a productive sense, not just for procreation but to enhance the creativity of humanity. This, of course, allows greater resonance within the womb and the seed, allowing a different creativity, a different child to be born. There will always be pleasure in the union between two people, but the pleasure involved in the future will not be just for self-gratification, it will be part of the union which you now begin to feel with the whole cosmos. You can therefore say that the pleasure derived from the union of two people will surpass any feeling that has so far been experienced.

The sacral chakra centre is an important energy centre. It always has been and will continue to be, because it is the spring-board for other forces within. The lower centre which you commonly call the base centre, will continue to be a vibrant force in its true state. The colour will alter, however. By this we mean the frequency or the note has altered, allowing the accommodation of greater communion with all that physically resides within you. We mean, of course, a connection with the earth, where you are. Therefore there is a true co-operation of energy between all that exists in matter. In the same way as there is a true co-operation on the higher planes. This is an important change for you. In a way it discontinues the very individualised state of each of you. Each person will continue to be unique, to have their own unique pattern, their unique range of possibilities, of permutations of the resonant frequencies already described. But the knowing connection to the whole now allows for a co-operation, a friendship and a union of energy forces that becomes very much part of the whole, although it continues its uniqueness.

You will be keeping your physical state, and that will only be made possible by the resonance of true joy entering not only the spirit of each person but the very cells of their being, allowing a positive and negative frequency to exist within one cell without a fight, repelling and attracting in one. The very repellent aspects of these differences will create the magnetism, and this will be discovered in time by your scientific fraternity.

Your cells have already changed allowing this accommodation of light. The willingness to change, the willingness to move forward without fear, must be present within the individual to accommodate the higher consciousness range within the body.

So the warmth and the beauty of love that creates this sound is a colour resonance of joy, made possible by the raising of energy from the heart, through and into the throat, registering just above the heart – which is what you rightly call the 'spirit level'. This creates a possibility never before imagined, not even by your greatest artists or innovators. However, many wise beings have sensed the enormity of possibilities that are now so perfectly within your range.

Fear is dissolving on a cellular level, even within those who think it has not gone. You hold within yourselves a memory of fear, but once you knowingly walk just a few steps without that fear, the memory and pattern fade and the DNA begins to alter.

There are different types of fear. There is a fear, which we have already mentioned, that is connected to the cells, to your whole structure and is impregnated within the cells. This fear is a kind of mutant in the cell. But what you can achieve now is a radiant cell, void and changed from its mutant state.

When you breed animals, or when you work to change plants, creating new colours and flowers, it is done over many generations. You can see the change as you bring out one aspect that you want to develop, and over a few generations this is created within its cellular memory. But the cellular change we are speaking of within humanity needs no further generation – it will be created through your joy. This answers many of your questions sent up to the higher planes.

You are becoming aware of this, aware of how you can use it, and the possibilities for using this to heal and help others. And of course that possibility exists, but recognise, with deep humility, that you cannot wave a magic wand for others. You can only help and inspire others to find their joy, through true love and an open heart – the heart that must never close now. And through your open heart, you can help them to expand. No visualisation or meditation can do this for another human being. Some positive thought-force will emanate from meditation, but to imagine you can give people a meditation or visualisation to change their DNA structure is incorrect. This change can only be achieved by the sound and resonance of the energy we speak of – joy – which is the resonance of love. Love in its highest form, through an open heart that can never be closed, is the only way, followed by the greatest will of all of you to expand.

Many of you have often wondered if your human state was some kind of experiment brought about by a crazy god. Indeed your lives are an experiment, and the crazy god is you! Besides, the experiment is reaching a point beyond anything that could have ever been imagined. We are all stepping into uncharted waters. Every human being treads where it has not been before. The constituents are the same, but the pattern changes once again, bringing new information, experience, strength and further power to the already powerful god-force to which you all belong. You are at one.

God the Father does exist. But god the children, which is you, also exists. Who can say who is more important, the Father or the Son? To the father the son may be more important, to the son the father. The giving and taking of love creates a holy spirit. The radiance and resonance that sends energy like shock waves out into the universe, creating yet more possibilities and more children in different forms. So do not be afraid when you see that some of those on your planet have unfortunately not taken this wonderful and marvellous opportunity. Their god soul-force lives on also. In a way the experiment of the earth as it has been, has now come to an end. Much has been learnt, many statistics and much information have formulated within the mind of God. We put away that experiment now as the transmutation and transformation of the new man begin.

When one soul has a truly open heart it is infectious to those who are within range. To simplify: the auric range is very wide in these individuals, and there are many of them, to a lesser or greater extent, who create radiance.

Some do one kind of work, some do another. There is no set way of resounding that light force, the light force of pure joy. It is merely an exchange and should someone of an expanded heart give a meditation or visualisation, it would help but that in itself would not make another individual change – the change only comes from the resonance of the true source.

You have a need to communicate and the meditational exercises that many of you are involved with, are a form of communication, but you already know there is a higher form of communication that goes beyond words and beyond visualisation. We cannot say, "Stop doing these things", because they enable the individual to feel safe, to touch their own energy, which in turn enables an opening of their true heart. But it is not the meditation in itself that opens the heart. There was a time when deep meditation was believed to be the only way to God and it is true that some forms of meditational exercises did allow wondrous capabilities, but they did not bring that individual to the closeness of God – it was only the true desire and the will of that individual that opened their hearts and then brought them into their true god-state.

It does not matter how you formulate your thoughts. It does not matter what you do. You have been brought up to believe that 'doing' is the purpose, and it is hard to erase these thoughts and beliefs. But 'doing' is not the purpose. The purpose is to grow and expand. Expansion comes from a true and open heart.

It is joyous to meditate. It is good to form groups and be in the energy of group meditation. Moreover, the healing work done within that does have its range and has played its part. But what we now speak of is that you, finally, have to come from that place of true inner willingness and knowingness that God is a real possibility.

Do not despair, everything you have done is loved. Everything you have ever been is loved. And everything you can be is loved, and when you recognise that, you know your part and your purpose.

You are becoming light beings, which is an excellent description brought from enlightenment and joy. We try to look for ways to describe this, all of which are inadequate, but we speak of an analogy that is not unknown to you: that is, of the tiny insect's perception of the great mammal. How do the ant and the elephant perceive each other? Do they perceive each other as they really are? Do they really know that each of them belongs to the same family, the same union and the same greater soul, with differences and different ways? Even the hard ways of negativity and fear lead the soul eventually back to all that is. We offer you that thought.

Chapter 8

Spiritual Union

We have been talking about the material of spirit, we now speak of spirit/matter. It is a form, unseen by your human eye, but it does exist. It is unseen because, in the past, its frequency has not been aligned to your particular kind of bodies, or at least to the acceptance of the realisation of spirit. In other words, this perception of spirit/matter can be seen, can be realised by a shift, an opening of the doors within the mind.

To open the doors within your mind, your whole being has to accept, not through faith, but total realisation and total knowing, that spirit/matter does exist; and this only comes about by heightened consciousness. You are seeing this now, even in the dullest of minds. Sometimes it is seen more clearly by a simple, uncluttered mind. It is harder to be perceived by a busy mind, one that busies itself with physical concerns. The value of speaking about spirit/matter is very important. We have said, and it is happening, that science and the medics will come to this in their own way. The higher planes are working to help this happen, so there can be an amalgamation of knowledge with the mystics, the medics and everyone. All it requires is for human beings to let go of the idea that they can be ridiculed for their knowing, and they may find that everyone shares this knowledge, because it comes from a deeper awareness. This is why intellectual conversations do not help. There is no proof in matter alone, but there is proof in spirit/matter, and there is proof within the inner higher mind, the knowing mind, and it is to this that all of you aspire and connect.

The spirit is the force that guides, pushes, expands and radiates within. It has its own purpose as well as allowing you to be alive in matter and alive in spirit. There is a dance of the different layers within. Spirit comes down and becomes matter. Moving through the dimensions is rather like coming down a ladder, with spirit at the top, and as you come further and further down, your perceptions become more solid in physical terms until you have solid physical matter (e.g. gases changing to water and then to ice). But physical matter is not a different substance. Think of this like a chemical reaction, in which all substances are from the same initial substance, since they are all one.

We give you this image of coming down the ladder because it serves well. We could talk about walking on a hillside or mountain, and from there, seeing things differently. We have spoken of this different perspective before, but it is important that you now recognise the true spirituality of mankind. This is not a belief system, this is not a religion, this is actual spirit/matter. It does exist. It is not solid, in your terms of solidity, but it has solidity in its own force, and by accepting that you automatically link to your spirit being, and as you link to your spirit being, you lift yourselves into new consciousness. Through the new consciousness you transform to become the new beings of light that you have already begun to realise is possible. In this, there are many processes of movement, many processes of awareness.

Beings of Light have worked through the spiritual planes helping humanity throughout the eons and they have been both agreeably surprised and sometimes disappointed, because many of you have chosen to continue going around the wheel of karmic experiences connected only with matter. The whole point of the karmic experiences was to realise your full potential of spirit/matter – god-man. It is very hard for you to fully understand through words what we are expressing, but through these words we will give the essence of spirit, and through the essence of spirit you will know. This is not just for those who have been aware of spiritual truths, or those who are well-read or well-versed in the mystic schools. It is truly for everyone because you all exist in spirit/matter.

When we said that meditation and thought will not, in themselves, create the new man, it was to this we were referring. The acknowledgement of the spirit allows the connection, and through the radiation of that connection you can use your thoughts to create new patterns and dissolve old ones. But until that point of true connection, thought and meditation in themselves will do little other than, of course, allow your connection with your inner selves and your inner peace. The peace can help untie and loosen your hold on matter. We suggest that you now accept your spirituality which is your true destiny.

This connects with what we have been trying to put

across to you in terms of your lower centres. The lower centres are connected with the physical being and the idea of the amalgamation and the unison of the higher spirit with the lower energies is important, because your connection with light is your true connection with spirit. Light is a force, and that force, as it enters matter, becomes extraordinary.

As the spirit energy comes through the higher centres it first of all enters the heart, then moves into the solar plexus, enabling a solidity of energy. This spiritual ray then permeates and amalgamates the sacral and the base centres. These are different energies to the solar plexus energy and always have been and will continue to be so. Instead of losing all the energy from the sacral centre (as is happening with the solar plexus energy, which is being replaced by the finer sunlight quality), you will not lose the actual force and power that always reside within that centre. But you will certainly lose all the negative energies, all the fear-based patterning including those in the cells and the imprinting of the fear within your genetic patterning, your DNA.

The force in this centre will then become extraordinarily powerful and this power will be very prominent. It will emanate and rise up through and into the higher chakra centres, making a particular connection with the higher intuition which is in the chakras of the third eye and crown centre. So this force, which is pure force, pure power, becomes the impetus, the power, the rocket that fuels the higher centres and the highest possibilities. It becomes the 'magic' which will then create, by your thoughts, the new ray, the new world and the new bodies of man. This can only occur when the heart is open and when the solar plexus is full of the clear sunlight compassion energy, because the solar plexus is a ceiling protection for the lower sacral, or sexual centre – it always has been.

The protection of compassion and of sympathy for your fellow man has been your protection against the animal instinct which creates possible violence and aggression, and those who did not have compassion were very often abusers. The solar plexus has always been the umbrella for the lower centres, and it now becomes more so because without the finer qualities and emanations of the solar plexus rays, you cannot get the pure force – it will not exist and it will not happen without the solar plexus clearance.

Mankind has been afraid of power, because power in itself, without that umbrella of the solar plexus centre, has been a destructive influence, but true power, true force is non-destructive. It is pure. It cannot destroy because it has no negativity, it has no desire to destroy.

The desires now, as man reaches this point of evolution, are totally at one with his spiritual union. You have in the past been opposed to desire as it was always assumed to be selfish, but your desires are absolutely what you should follow, because, aligned to higher consciousness, they become the true spiritual desires, connected with the God-force, therefore connected to light. This is why the sacral centre is important. The true energy of this centre gives the possibility of creation and productivity, not just the procreation of races, but the furtherment of your evolution and the creativity of further knowledge through that evolution.

This does not mean you will not have procreation through sexuality. You will still have genders, although genders as you understand them will become very much less defined, and you will still have sexual union between a man and a woman. This union, with this true force, will be a giving force, a creative force, not just for the procreation of the new human being, but the new force that will allow its own to be born out of the higher planes. The connections and union between light beings will not be a gratification of sexuality but an energy that creates children on the higher planes. It will create thoughts and power on the higher planes enabling a radiance of the higher consciousness.

When some of you get carried away with ideas of connecting with other stars and galaxies, you are looking at it from the wrong angle. You are now aware of the connection (not that it hasn't been there before), and this awareness creates curiosity. Curiosity allows you to reach forward, but you are already connected – not just from one place, but from all places. Many of you have had existences in places beyond your globe, beyond your planet and galaxy, in different stars and different places, and of course those stars themselves have come initially from the same original substance.

You will not learn anything more by endeavouring to link with a specific star, or a specific star cluster other than the memory that has gone before, not just for one person, but for all of mankind because there have been physical, mental and, of course, spiritual connections to particular areas of the cosmos. These connections have now become memories that are being awakened in you, just as the awakened memory happens when you remember your own karmic journey, your own past existences.

But every person is part of each other, and an experience for one is an experience for all. This is only found out through having different bodies through incarnations. However, the different bodies ultimately do not exist, they are just a form which allows experiences unique within themselves, individual within themselves but part of the whole. The higher memory, the higher consciousness is connected to all beings and all life forms wherever they dwell, and however you perceive them.

At one particular stage of evolution it is not possible to have full comprehension of all of this because it would be too much and it would not allow you particular growth, in particular ways. This is why you think you have forgotten, but in truth, you have forgotten nothing because the memory still exists in your consciousness. However, the memory of negativities and fear must be lost, not in terms of memory, but in terms of your connections with it. This is a difficult concept for you: to be able to remember it without connection. As your mind exists now you could not comprehend everything that has been and will be, and yet, within the higher mind you have the knowledge of all that is, or was, or will be.

You will access what you need at this time because it is appropriate to you, and you will also be able then, by your greater understanding, to comprehend. It is rather like expecting a baby to understand a scientific equation when it cannot speak properly. But in time, as the baby grows and learns, it understands. And so it is with you and your understanding of greater things.

There are beings who exist in dimensions that you never see who also have limited views of their own dimensional state. They do not see you as you see yourselves, although they may have some conscious awareness of you. They exist in their own time and space. The whole cosmos and the whole state of life is beyond your imagining and the permutations of these light forms are beyond anything you can fully realise.

We come back now to the heart energy. We particularly want to emphasise that this is not an idealised attitude of perfected love, nebulous as an ideal or an expectation. It is an actuality. Heart energy is what you call unconditional love. It is unconditional, it is not an ideal, nor is it a hope. It does exist! It is a heart-ray energy force which is the central line of balance of all forces – the middle path, the middle way. It holds the positive and negative energies of the whole cosmos. By this we do not mean the negative destructive energy, we mean the male and female energy as you understand it. It is the heart-ray that holds those forces, acting as the bridge. It is fundamental to your total acknowledgement and 'being' of the true spirit/matter.

You will perhaps best access this understanding through the openness of this heart energy, because that offers you the middle line, the middle way through which you can perceive both sides. By standing on that middle line you can experience the unconditional love state, and through the unconditional love state you can see your true potential as spirit/matter – god-man. This is why the emphasis is on working with the heart at this time. It is not expectation, hope, faith, nor is it a religion, although the true essence of love is within all teachings. We speak of being 'at the heart of the matter' and by being in the heart you are with matter and with spirit.

This is not something that can be taught through words, however pure the channelling or the channeller. It must come from within each individual, through their deeper understanding. Most of you will have already had some understanding of this. Most of what we speak of will just emphasise one particular aspect and will confirm what is already in your deeper, higher mind. These words are not for reassurance, but they will reassure. It is to help you reach your fullest, truest potential which has no end, but in its higher states, is just beginning!

What we speak of is not nebulous, it is as solid in its actuality and reality as solid earth beneath your feet. It will be realised by all of you because time is running out and everyone is being 'pushed into the corner'. And by being pushed into a corner you are forced to accept a greater view, a greater potential for enlightenment. That time is now!

Chapter 9

The Soul Mind

Most of humanity is going through the motion of living their lives with old patterns, mainly out of habit, out of memory. But in reality the energy of today is not in line with these old thought patterns, which will not be able to manifest in matter for very much longer. There will be a lot of confusion for many people as they begin to realise that their lives are totally without foundation and without any point. This will have an enormous effect on all areas of modern life. It will be frightening because a lot of people will feel insecure. They will try to hang on to things outside themselves, and for very short periods dictators and those who want power over others could establish some kind of zombie-army because these people do not understand and have no connection with their inner force.

So a time is coming when you will see the break-down of society in many areas. Different nations and different people will react differently depending on their own vibrational ray. If they have not allowed the violence within their genetic and cultural ray to dissolve, there will be much more violence. Do not, however, be alarmed by this because it will only be in pockets and will be very, very quickly cleared. It will only last a short period of time, but nonetheless it will be a dangerous time; it is as well to be very attuned to your own intuitive forces so you will know where to be and what to be doing so that, as these destructive energies manifest, you can avoid them.

All the energies within your body are changing. We have spoken about this, but we would now like to speak about the changing mind, for, as the energy system within the body changes and takes on new energy, swopping the old for the new, it affects every area of the body. The way the body reacts to this is different to the way the mind reacts.

The intellectual mind is still working but is beginning to function as a secondary mind. We have to speak now in terms that are not absolute. When we speak of a higher mind, we speak of a greater mind. We speak, therefore, of the soul-mind. This is not the same mind as the intellectual mind, but it has a thinking process and an energetic force.

The soul-mind is now activated and will take over from the intellect. Therefore the way you think will radically alter – you will not reason in logical ways, you will only use the lower intellectual mind for logical thinking, but all major decision making activities, and all major responses for knowledge and curiosity of knowledge, will come from the higher mind – the soul mind.

This is important for you to understand because many of you have already made the shift from the intellectual mind to what we will now define as the intuitive state.

This is not the same as a psychic experience – our difficulty is in giving you words that you can understand. It is a psychic experience in as much as you cannot see it with your three-dimensional senses, although the third-dimensional senses are expanding as well. The higher mind is joined to the intuitive knowledge even though the latter feels as though it is isolated. It does not need data, facts and figures like your intellectual mind nor does it need reason, but it does need some input, some stimulant. So an ordinary thought joined to the intuitive aspect of yourselves will set in motion a sense, a knowing, a being state, that allows you to know what needs to be done, what knowledge you have and this will then be re-translated to the intellectual mind. This is how it is occurring at the moment.

Some people have already shifted so that the intuitive mind, the greater mind is working all on its own. It does not need seed thoughts, it senses in ways that are not three-dimensional. It senses, and it knows that you feel these things conceptually although you do not know how they are being translated. You will hear many people saying, "I don't know how I knew that, I don't know how I came to that conclusion," or "I don't know why I made this decision," and yet – and this is the dilemma of language – it came from the true knowing, the knowing within. If this seems rather complicated it is only because we are having to describe this through the intellectual sources which do not comprehend the higher mind, so we can only use comparable language to give you some idea of what this means.

The accessing of the higher mind has, in the past, been done by sending a seed-thought from the intellectual mind, which was translated by the higher mind, then translated again as the thought was passed back to the intellectual mind, and in translation much was lost. You cannot acknowledge by touch, sight, hearing or any other stimulus from your human mind, the higher mind. Now, however, some of you are by-passing the intellectual input and are working directly from the higher mind. This means that, intellectually, there is no energy, no input or output, and the knowing comes from a sensing, a knowing, but not from the intellect. This is a difficult concept to put across because of its complexity, but we will explain this in detail because it needs to be understood as many people are beginning to work on this different level and yet feel they are somehow unable to justify this, unable to work properly, or unable to describe it or reason with it. There is a reasoning involved, and it has nothing to do with logic. The reasoning is purely the higher reasoning and this is an enormous step for humanity to take. For so long your medical and scientific fraternity thought that intellect was the greatest aspect of the human animal, but it is not. Spirit and the soul are the greatest aspects. It is true that intellect has allowed you to have many experiences to reason, to enjoy, to fear and to push forward, but mankind's intellect has reached its ceiling. There is nowhere else for it to go.

You are now fulfilling a destiny of humanity transmuting into a different being, not unintelligent and not abandoning the intellect, but allowing a destiny that mankind's intellect will infuse within the soul-force. The mystics among you will understand the soul-infused personality – the emotions infused within the soul – but you have not given much consideration to the infusing mind. This is a very important factor in your growth, and one which means that the form of channelled communication we are sharing together will become defunct because the intuition, the higher mind, will 'know' and will not need outer information.

This intuitive state – when fully formed, and when you are fully fledged within it – means that you will work quite differently. You will work with a synchronisation that is now unknown. You will know what to do and where to be, not by your desire and certainly not by your reason, but by your knowing. This is not the same as an animal instinct, which is only a lower form of survival, even though the best word to use is 'instinctual'. It is an instinctual response to the knowledge within. In time, this will focus itself, not as an intellectual piece of information, but as a piece of information fully lodged within your being.

It will be as if you are walking into an enormous self-perpetuating mind with all knowledge of all times. The extraordinary thing about this is that you will keep your body. This higher mind-state is rarely used within physical substance or matter. Yet you will be working with matter, your human body, your spirit and soul, all at the same time. This occurrence in human form has not been achieved before, en masse. It has been achieved only by a very few, for specific reasons, throughout history.

So you are special beings of light and you are metamorphosing! Although for a long time you will look very similar to the way you look now, you will not be the same. You will be working from a different point and focus. You will be working almost without reason, and yet, you will be propelling the evolutionary process to very high levels. To manage this your bodies are having to restructure, and your DNA structure is already changing. Your planet is also changing radically and, in a very short space of time, you will not know it as the same world.

Although Earth itself is changing its consciousness and the land on which you live will be quite different, for the time being anyway it will look reasonably similar. Be careful, because during this transition between the lower and higher mind, there will be much fear. Fear because of a lack of security brought about by misunderstanding and even those who know about the changes may put the wrong connotations on to them. This has nothing to do with judgement, it is not about some benevolent God saying that humanity has been good, or it has not, or it deserves this or that. It is simply about cause and effect. But cause and effect are moving into a new area. The whole cosmos is cause and effect, the whole cosmos breathes in and breathes out, but very few places work in the same way as your planet, with matter and spirit working together.

The experience the human being is about to encounter has only been made possible by the continuous strengthening of the genes and cells within the body. It is this continuous movement and strengthening of the human being on all levels that have enabled him to take this step. But most importantly, it is because humanity now desires it, for without desire, true desire, this could not take place.

We could put all this in scientific terms and have previously made some attempts to do so; but in scientific terms it does not really mean anything as it does not resonate with the scientist. So we speak to the heart, to the knowing and the higher mind that you all are about to use. To live on your world in the future you will need to work from the higher mind. It will not be possible to work just from the human mind – and many, many of you are able to make this transition.

Trust the process out of your own knowing. We are not asking anyone to trust without that knowing, we are not asking for blind, ignorant faith; we are asking you to touch what you know to be true within and to begin to work more fully with it. There is, of course, a great struggle with these old habits; the habits, not just of a lifetime, but of hundreds of lifetimes. We are suggesting that you use a different instrument, a very different instrument as your focal point for the future. This is not an easy thing to do and although the transition has been coming over a very long period of time, longer than any of you realise, there still needs to be a point of departure. With most people fortunately it has come swiftly, easily and fairly fluidly, but as you continue now, if you are going to make this leap, it has to be done very quickly. For those who make this leap into the future, the systems within your body will jar and jolt, which will affect the nervous system, the immune system and all those aspects that are resistant to change. Of course, this cannot be done in an emotional state and this is why we have spoken so much about the dissolution of fear. Your bodies are very mutable, they are very adaptable, much more adaptable than you realise, and the latent qualities of the use of this higher mind have always been possible. It is one of the many permutations of the evolutionary process. Now it is time to make this leap. The previous evolutionary leap, made by instinctual animal to the intellectual mind, was a great step, but it is not a fraction of the leap you are going to make now.

Your intellectual minds will not be redundant, they will be utilised and infused within the deeper self, and for some specific purposes they will act like magic formulas, sending out to the higher mind an energy that will be able to manifest a thought immediately. These are things you could previously only have dreamed of. This is far beyond anything you have seen on your films and in books, and beyond anything from the most imaginative of minds. The most wonderful opportunity and experience are coming.

For those of you who have been slightly concerned that there would be nothing to do, we assure you that in the new world there will be much to do. Your purpose, therefore, is to take this challenge and move with it willingly.

Everything on your planet mirrors everything else. Scientists are discovering things that have always been there. But they are being discovered now because they are mirroring humanity's growth and thoughts.

There is an extraordinary connection between everything. When there is knowledge of any description, it goes out on the ethers to every consciousness, so anything discovered on any level is known by all. There is an enormous synchronisation therefore as one aspect of life mirrors another. There is a huge symphony taking place constantly, permanently. Everything follows on from everything else. Everything flows beautifully in the whole cosmos. When something is newly discovered, the realisation sets about a process of manifestation within the human framework, although only a few know about it. The realisation of these different possibilities creates movement, change and further knowledge. Everything perpetuates every other thing. There is no end, there is only movement, but the realisation of this at an intellectual level is unimportant compared with the realisation of the higher mind and all possibilities involved with the communication of that. By being in total communication and total unison with the higher mind, the human being transcends, transforms, emerges from its prison to become a winged creature within its own heart, flying to places as yet unseen.

There are no exercises or formulas for contacting the higher mind, but the sum total of all the experiences felt, coupled with the changes of your world and the cosmos, have brought together this possibility. It is not just possible, it is beginning to occur. Be very happy with all this because it truly means the end of suffering, as you understand suffering, the end of struggle, and the beginning of unimaginable knowledge.

Chapter 10

Use Your Magic!

The importance of this channelling work is unknown to you. There is the very real probability of channelling ending because all of you will be able to intuitively reach your own information. But as with any piece of information, when it hits a consciousness, even if it is only one consciousness, it radiates and expands, it becomes manifest. So when channelling comes into actuality through the spoken word, it permeates through the mind of all humanity. It creates an energy of realisation, not on a logical or factual level, but it becomes part of your dream world, and as it does, it begins to manifest in matter. Everything mirrors everything else, and everything is part of everything else, but to bring actuality – materialisations of the cosmos – down into matter, it needs to seep through different layers of consciousness landing within the human mind. As it lands within the human mind it then takes place within the human state.

Within the physical, inventions have occurred

simultaneously in different parts of your world even before your communications were set up, even before your telegraph and your telephone installations, long before satellites. Two people or more invent the same thing, have the same knowledge, at the same time. This has come about through the consciousness of people being at one and by the lowering of the higher consciousness, through the physical being, through the dream state, and into the human conscious mind.

This is the purpose of the channelling, to create the higher world in matter. It has always occurred but it has occurred slowly, rather like water in a sponge, slowly seeping in through different layers, sometimes painfully seeping into the consciousness. Now it is able to come clearly through many channellers, indeed, all can be and will be channellers. But at this time when your history is speeding up, it is important to understand that even if you have no connection to various areas of society, you can now connect with them automatically through the consciousness state, the collective mind-state. This will create a higher consciousness state from the actuality of the connection of the conscious mind. It is true, therefore, that one thought in one mind is everyone's thought in all minds.

We could describe this higher consciousness as a satellite, and you now have the 'equipment' to link with that satellite. Therefore you can access information that has not been accessible to most of you in the past, although a few of you have been able to tap into that information. It truly is a time of communication in ways, and by means, that you do not yet see.

As this information seeps down into the conscious mind it needs to create its own process within the individual because what can be learnt intellectually, even academically, needs to be proven within the material state. This is also happening with remarkably little frustration. In the past, man was frustrated by the higher and the lower mind. Now there is less frustration because man is beginning to accept his higher intuitive state.

It is very important that all people accept the intuitive state on whatever level they can, even if they just accept the instinctive psychic level that is animal in its quality. For that acceptance allows them to tune to their higher mind, to their soul self and that sets off the reverberation of light within the individual. This shifts their own difficulties, their fears, enabling them now to access through the throat areas of communication intuitive states of the crown and third eye centres. When you understand this, you will understand the necessity for clearing the lower chakra levels, which is a paramount step to the change in your evolution.

Intuitional radiance is paramount to your sense of direction. Some have felt directionless, but as they begin to connect to their intuitional radiance, this will help them. And the force behind that intuitional radiance is pure magic!

The intuitive centres in the head will look after themselves if they have the impetus, the energy from deep within to get this purification of energy. The old stuff, as you refer to it, has to be removed. We must emphasise this is not emotional, and although we talk of fear, it is not emotional fear as you understand that to be. Every single part of your structure has accumulated its energy through experience, and the evolution of all living things takes place through that experience. If the climate changes, the body changes, because it needs to, in order to survive. It is an automatic process. But because man has been ill-equipped and unable to let go of his fear, this fear has expanded, seeping into the emotional chakra centre, creating all the problems that have been encountered as a result. Although this was never intended, it has had the added bonus of bringing you the sort of experiences that, perhaps, could not have been envisaged and that have strengthened you in a way that other beings in other universes have not been strengthened.

Now it is time for your impregnated cellular fear, which is different from the emotional fear, to be cleansed. As you already know, this is not done through meditation, however powerful, but by the sheer willingness to simply let go. It is achieved by willingness, and the will, through the connection of honesty, integrity and the absolute commitment to truth within you. This will allow you to open up to clean the solar plexus centre, to enable the light-force to impregnate.

Listen to the word 'impregnate'. Conceive within the sacral centre the conception of light. In this conception of light, the cells that are then made within that area enlighten and can help the birthing process of the new humanity; the impregnation of light within the cells dissolves, burns up, clears and purifies all that is remnant of the 'old stuff'. This is why your dreams, your expectations, your acknowledgement of light, and the possibilities that light creates, are paramount to the birth of the new child.

Much work has been done on the new child. You are dreaming the creation of the new being, who will be resonant in their strength, and able to be independent immediately at birth. You will very soon have a state when your new-born babies will not need to be suckled for any great length of time. They will stand on their feet very quickly, because they will have no dependency. They are born with their own independency of light. This will discontinue some of the old tasks of women. The female energy is of great importance, as indeed so is the male, for together you infuse in light the god-force, the holy spirit, the trinity of energy creating the oneness, and you simply cannot have the oneness without the connection of the duality of energies. This mystical information is becoming known to you on a very deep level, so the clearance of the sacral energy, clearing out the debris of the past, gives you the real meaning of the power of man. This power, which has been wrapped in the sexual areas, will now be extended and aligned with the spiritual. This will raise the power-energy and the instrument of the true erection of energies that is within you all, male or female. This will ignite the lower flame of sacral energies beyond the lower desires, yet the will and the true desire of spiritual progression when a child is requested, will now occur in a very moving way and be a beautiful experience.

The ignited flame will soar through the chakra centre that has no blocks. The flame that tried to move up through blocks created an unhealthy experience, and the energy imploded back on itself, creating what might be termed soot and dirt within the lower areas. But now the flame will flow through the body, like flowing up a chimney, moving through the solar plexus, ignited and alighted by the heart, moving up to the throat and touching the intuitive energies in the head. Through the combination of the intuitive energies and the sacral flames you have true manifestations of desires.

Desire is not wrong when it is attuned to love. You have the desire that creates the dreams that now create matter.

You are able to have a situation whereby the higher consciousness, instead of coming down from the higher planes and being received by you, actually comes from within you, turning it into a positive action. The actuality of the dreams also now comes from within you, not from beyond. The only reason in the past that the higher consciousness came from beyond you was because of blocks. The coming down of higher consciousness was receptive, the coming from within is positive, so you now begin to have the true union within the body, within the chakra centres vibrating in light, and the true union of the mother/father/child/holy spirit/god-force. Because of this, it may be relevant and possible for human beings to procreate within themselves. But that is for another time, a further place, and need not concern you now.

When a movement is made, it changes all movements. One tiny movement changes the possibilities of the future. The possibilities of the future are enormous and as you begin to move into the higher consciousness levels, you understand possibilities that are immense and yet you are unconnected to what occurs because you know that you are safe.

You have archetypal images of men and women with wands. This is symbolic of the union of which we have spoken and the magic wand is an actuality of the union of the forces. This is why even some time ago, we told you to be careful of your thoughts, because even before the fusion of these forces, the thoughts were beginning to take action and to become magic.

Having ignited the flame there will then be no block to total connection with the oneness of spirit and the oneness of all humanity. Do not see yourselves as inferior – you are not inferior to God. You and your potential are one with God and the realisation of that oneness is what will allow the fully fledged energy of the earth and spirit to merge as one. Then you will see the change, the physical change in man because the base chakra centre deals with the energy of the pure physical flesh, and as the oneness of creation occurs between the flames of the sexual centre and the intuitive magic, you can literally create the body that you want.

You are already beginning to talk about light bodies, star-like bodies, transparent bodies. It is already seeping into your consciousness that the evolutionary process is taking the human body further down the road, and, yes, you can live as long as you like. Your flesh and your bones are becoming light, literally, actually, light, and they are blending in harmony with the light-force. You will not, at this stage anyway, cut yourselves off from the physical body but you will use the physical state to experiment, to have adventures in time and space, both on your planet and on other planets. This will be the star child of the future. This star child will not come from the stars but from within the connection to light.

How quickly you have moved! Just consider how quickly your consciousness is changing, how quickly these shifts are creating this new human being. Your dreams will be helped by those beings who are already light. This you have control over. Nothing and no one will take your control from you. But you, at this point, are becoming one with light beings and therefore they are your brothers, your twin, and you totally accept and love them, and are guided by them. There is at this point total trust. This is coming gradually, yet quicker and quicker. Even your governments and political figures are beginning to mirror these higher manifestations.

There will be much talk about self-responsibility, which will be translated by some in a very mundane way, but it is the echo of the true self-responsibility within each individual. By being at one with God does not diminish your individuality, it enhances it, for you will know your union with all and, therefore, you become as one with all.

You can feel and touch the physical movement of energy within a tree because trees are living entities that are echoing your transformation. Watch the trees and listen to their silent stillness that is not without action. There is nothing in the whole cosmos that does not have action, even within the whole mind of God, the still consciousness of the God/soul force, there is action. This is the dichotomy for you, that even in the stillness there is movement and in movement there is stillness. And in your movement there will be stillness.

Look at how much you physically do. Look how much you get done within one day. Look how fast your time seems to be running. Yet you are still. You are whole. You are the same within that movement, within that time and space. You are already one!

Begin to use your magic, begin to use your beam. Begin to use your intuition, consciously, positively. You can do no wrong. You will not misuse your power because your desire to goodness will not allow you to do so. Do not be afraid of using your new-found power. Do not be fearful, even when others may criticise. You have knowledge of fire and through that knowledge of fire you have power. Are you going to deny your whole world that knowledge out of fear, out of ideals, out of criticism? Use your magic!

Chapter 11

The Centre of Equilibrium

Hear the words you need in your hearts. Learn to listen, this is the challenge. Not to listen outside but to listen inside. You have been trained, in terms of hearing, to block off extraneous noises of traffic, aeroplanes, people who annoy you. You block away those things, so consequently the true art of listening is not something that many of you can touch. Listening from that cool inner silence, listening and being connected to that inner silence allows you not to hear words, but to know – conceptually know – what you need to do, where you need to be and who you really are at any given time. This knowing then communicates itself via your third eye to your brain, which then translates it into the conscious mind.

A series of layers – a series of roads, and little inlets in the roads – within yourselves has to be circumnavigated for the energies to hit your conscious mind. Obviously within that process, if there is an imbalance, or any kind of denial, or blocks, which there usually are, then the focus of that information translates itself incorrectly to the human state. Do not worry about this because you seem to be able, despite this, to feel and sense your way and in time you are able to connect to the true message. Although this may sound a somewhat clumsy process, it actually happens at the speed of light. So the intuitive mind, the intuitive state, is important as a receiver of the true knowing within.

Information does not come to the intuitive mind, it comes through the higher mind. It is the intuitive state that receives it and translates it to the conscious mind. You have different words for this. Psychologists call this the subconscious and you have created elaborate identifications for this, particularly in the last 50 to 100 years when some people have tried to intellectualise it. A whole process of awareness has been built up on the discovery of these layers of the Self. In one way, there is no need for you to understand it, although it is always helpful to understand or to realise that there is a process.

To polish your instrument of the intuitive mind is an excellent thing to do because, when you receive information, it then has a 'clearer run'. To do this, you need to have a clear, resonant heart, and a clear resonant energy from the lower chakra centres, particularly from the energy-link of the lower base, sacral centre which, free in its true state, polishes, clears and purifies all the other centres and gives energy an impetus to the third eye region. The side effect of this now is that many people are discovering their intuitive state, their natural psychic faculties. The danger of this discovery, depending on the individual, is that they can go off at a tangent assuming it means something else.

One of the great assumptions that many humans have

made is that you are somehow unique because of your psychic abilities or because you have a special purpose given by God. All of you have a special purpose given by God. All of you have God within. This assumption on your behalf is because you have nothing to understand it by consciously, but if only you took the time to come into a listening state, you would then discover your true potential and realise that it is unique, yes, because you are all unique, and everyone is joined to the higher mind.

The energy area that you use most to listen with, in energy terms, is of course the throat. As the 'spirit level' of man is moving from the heart to the throat, the energy of the throat is fundamentally important to the new state of humanity. It is ironical that the listening centre is the energy that, when touched, enables you to perceive things beyond the human state, the third-dimensional state. You can then begin to perceive the higher mind and gradually, through the expansion of your own selves, discover the wealth of knowledge, its purpose and the living state within. You also begin to discover that all the things around you that are accepted as being solid, fast and unmoving, do move and have life. Everything has life. Everything has movement. It is the perception of the movement of everything around you that allows you to realise the higher possibilities that all of you now have.

You are waking up to the discovery of these possibilities. Not necessarily things that you are doing, but the discovery of things that are possible. Because there are no structures, the whole of life in the cosmos is a moving, living state, everything is movement, even you, as you sit on your chair. There is movement within. Your chair is moving and you are moving in time and space. You are moving even within your own dimensions, and there is movement within the flow of your cells and blood.

There is, in the whole cosmos, constant movement. The event of a comet colliding with Jupiter, in July 1994, was relatively small compared to other movements and changes. It was, for you, a great event, but such occurrences are not unusual. Nothing is static, nothing stays forever in one place. Your own planet is moving at great speed. It is moving on its own axis and it is moving through space.

You now have the ability to perceive these things, both scientifically and from a higher level. The movement of all affects everything, so as one thing moves it affects everything else. The comet hitting Jupiter is a perfect example, as it affects the delicate gaseous atmosphere around the planet. The explosions within the atmosphere affected the planet itself which shifted its trajectory very slightly, but even this slight trajectory movement affects everything else, and this movement has a knock-on effect. This will not happen immediately and indeed much of this will be forgotten before some influence is felt. The influences that were felt immediately were subtle, but even one tiny movement within the galaxy eventually affects everything else as it works itself through time and space.

The feeling of disorientation, the feeling of disassociation that many of you have had recently, is because you are recognising this fluid state on a deep level and sometimes that recognition comes before it hits the conscious. There is a feeling of disorientation even on a physical level. Many of you are asking, "What is it all about?" Many are confused. We say to you, do not be confused, be centred, be connected – listen – you will know, not from these words or even from any words given by any teacher or guide, but by your own resonance, by your own being. Why are so many of you reluctant to rely on yourselves when you have total independence of spirit, when you have everything you need? It is there for all of you. The connection is there. This is what we are trying to bring through to you now.

You have free will, but you are not recognising that your will works for you, if you allow it. Why do you allow yourselves to be blown around like leaves in the wind? Stability is within you. When we speak of stability we are not speaking of inertia, we are speaking of the feeling of being completely safe. Because you are safe. Use your whole life as a meditation – not as an altered state, but as a focus of being.

The changes within the structure of your planet are already occurring. There is much evidence on your planet of rain and water and in the early part of 1995, much flooding occurred all over the world. This is just one aspect of the atmospheric change that is occurring. The sun will also be brighter and because of the change of your atmosphere you will have to watch your skin, but this only needs your normal awareness.

We do not wish to predict other changes; anyway, nothing can be certain in terms of planetary shifts. If you throw a pack of cards in the air, you cannot be absolutely certain where one card will land! Movements and changing patterns are always in operation, which is why, particularly at this time when major shifts are likely on many levels, including structural shifts, it is so important for you to listen to yourselves, to be centred and to be safe within your centred state.

Understand that you are all free. You are not tied to this place and time. Experience, enjoy and love your human existence. The more you love your human state, the more you give to it, the more you can receive. The process of expansion is then greater, but you are not in any way trapped or caught within this third-dimensional plane.

Some people are feeling tired as a result of the many shifts. This tiredness will go for most of you, as it comes from the connection with the physical state. This is difficult to explain because we do not want you to assume that you will abandon your physical state, indeed, we emphasise, the physical state will continue, it will change, but it will continue. If you just focus yourselves within your centred, silent stillness you will find that your energy levels are much better than they have ever been. This will come in fits and starts. We understand your concern, but everything has its own way of equalising – human beings are no different – and you will equalise yourselves in energy terms.

The heart is the centre of this equilibrium. This is the reason why the heart centre is, at this time, so important. Although there is constant movement, everything is constantly balancing itself, so there is balance and movement, which may sound to you as though it is a contradiction, but it is not. It is both equal and opposite. It is the force of positive and negative, male and female, always constantly adjusting itself in its own equilibrium, and that is occurring within your own human bodies as well.

It is the balance of the lower and the higher forces, the spiritual and the physical, the unseen and the seen. The unseen is only unseen because most of you have not, as yet, opened up your instruments. But you are beginning to open them so some of the unseen is becoming seen very rapidly. Ironically, with the tiredness also comes a lack of concern, you could say that you no longer care. That is accurate in a lower state, a lower way of observing life. But the unconditional caring is taking over. So you care less for those things that you have worked with through the whole of your karmic existence, but you will care more about the greater things, the greater reality and the greater truths. So, whilst in living in your physical lives it feels for many of you as though you are becoming uncaring, you are not. You are in fact becoming more realistic in your own balanced state.

To help you, we offer you a thought: as you breathe, breathe air into your throats. Connect with the sky through your throat, connect with the energy of the open spaces and in that connection you will know that everything is infinite, that there is no end. No ceiling. No structure. In this way give yourselves love, draw in love. Hear and feel that love.

Chapter 12

The Overview

For those of you who think nothing is happening, let it be known that a very great deal is happening, moving and shifting. You are experiencing subtle but very real changes – within every part of every living cell. You are not the same as you were even twelve months ago, and the planet is not the same either. You have experienced time lapses, and you have also experienced the feeling of time speeding up. In reality, your time is slowing down, but what is reality? Reality is what you perceive. What you experience is reality. Many of you have been waiting for extraordinary physical movements. Yet extraordinary physical movements have already occurred and continue. They have occurred within the human body and they have occurred within plant life – different species have been born and others have disappeared.

To see all this, you need to have an overview, a greater perspective. The reason many of you cannot see is because you are only looking around your vicinity, and seeing without clarity. If you have an overview you can see the changes very clearly. Your waters are changing. We do not mean the flow of water, we mean the substance of water, the molecules within the water have changed and continue to change. Water is of paramount importance to you. It also shifts and grows, and the different molecules in the water are now changing the water you drink. The moisture that is absorbed through your skin is, in turn, changing the cells within your body.

Your hope for a better world will be realised. The world is getting better in your terms. We remind you however that your karmic world is not a world to 'make you better'. The karmic world is to give you experience. You have gone around the wheel of karma for experience, the by-product has been the build-up of what we refer to as spiritual muscle, but the purpose of the karmic world is not to be better or to build up spiritual muscle – it is to experience. Only by separation can you experience yourselves. One godhead has separated itself into trillions and trillions, countless different species – one of which is you – and in doing that the godhead experiences itself.

There are numerous combinations and possibilities of life. You are part of that godhead, and through the separation of the godhead you perceive greater aspects of yourselves. This is what is meant by a chosen experience. Each tiny cell is part of that whole. Each planet is part of that whole. Each sun, each solar system, each galaxy, everything that exists is part of the godhead. The difference now is that what your perception has recognised as, and what you have called, evil, is not evil, but is in reality good because the so-called evil has allowed experience to strengthen you. When you finally realise this you dissolve the separation, the polarity of good and bad, because in reality there is no such thing. In actuality, all comes from the whole. If you understand that your pain, your discomfort, your anxieties and even the horrific evil that you see around your planet, are part of this process, you can dissolve the feeling of evil. In that dissolution, you have the truth, and you can then leave your karmic experience and move forward into a greater, or different reality. Again we say, "Does the caterpillar know that one day it will be a butterfly, and does the butterfly remember it has been earth-bound as a caterpillar?"

There are many facets of what you call a diamond. Similarly, many of you are now perceiving frequencies of energies which were once unknown to you but which have always been present. You are perceiving energies in the earth. You are even perceiving energies in ordinary pebbles and stones which, not so very long ago, appeared to many of you as dead. You are awakening to the properties within that stone, to the energy of a simple pebble, you can link with and register the energies beneath your feet. You can communicate with these energies. They are your brothers. And in your communication, which is from both you and them, you will become more aware of possibilities which were beyond your thoughts even a few weeks ago. There are no limits!

Many of you have now experienced communication from those beyond your globe. They are part of the whole also, and there is joy, and sometimes pain, in these communications because there is lack of understanding. At times there is terror. But you will understand each other and you will grow in each other's presence as you communicate more fully to many more cosmic energies.

We want to inspire you to take an overview. We want to inspire you beyond the aspect of your pain, and all you have to do to relinquish the pain is to know that all is good. The time has come for suffering to end, and this is part of the clearance.

The trees in the forests of the world, sensitive as those great beings are, recognise the change. Their branches and leaves smell the changing currents of the air and the changing currents of energy. So if you truly want to observe your planet as a physical life force, all you have to do is observe your trees. Link with their energies and speak with them, they speak to you and they have much to say, although you do not need to know those things. All you need to know is that you are perfect as you are and however else you will be.

We have been very careful not to mislead you, not to allow you to take avenues and pathways that will take you away from the raising of your conscious awareness. Some people, with their impossible curiosity, dig, pick and probe; learn things and experience the difference of energies, and this is fine. But when these things take you down the road of fear by another name, then they are not good. Because the loosening of your fear is so immediate, it is too easy for you to fall into that trap. What we are speaking of is not about positive thought in itself, it is about positivity in your words. It is about experience.

We spoke before of being like children given matches, you may be burnt and some of you have been, whilst taken up with the enormity, the movement, imagining this or that needing to be done to protect and to save lives. Your lives are saved. How can you save something that will never die? All you do by this approach is to promote anxiety. Remember that the possibility of expansion is great, you can shift and rise beyond the mundane, remember these things with a clear clarion note but do not allow exaggeration to take you into untruths.

Sweet souls, do you not see that when you deal with another person, you are communicating with them. If you communicate to their light, to their essence, you allow the resonance of power and goodness to emerge. You do nothing by relating to the negativity and the fear; you hinder yourselves if you do. Each one of you must, within your own hearts, realise your possibilities, realise your power and use it. What good is power that is hidden? Use it to promote the magnetism of the light-force within another soul to emerge likewise.

Your world is being watched, it is fascinating to others' eyes. Just as sometimes you sit and watch a whole colony of ants, wondering at their strength, their purpose and their being, so you too are watched with gentle love in all the things you do. There is mystery in the things you do, and yet a perfect patterning is only seen from above as everything blends in perfectly, creating different colours in the kaleidoscope of your lives. Only by activating your mind beyond that, beyond yourselves, do you see who you truly are.

The irony of this is, when you see who you truly are, you then realise that your job is where you are, what you do now, in the moment. Some of you have had a sense of a world that has no time as you understand it. Some of you are already working on the new ray of living. Isn't it unbelievable that all you need is there for you?

Your world has changed. It is impossible to live with the old time. Your new world has already begun and the start of a new race has occurred. Those of you who have taken this challenge to be here on earth at this time will see the wonder of the new birth!

Be clear in your mind. It may feel strange not to be attached to the experience of karma, it may feel as though you have lost something. You have not lost it, but it has gone. Where is the struggle? Where is the purpose?

The Purpose is You

The purpose is your continued experience within a different time-span, dimension and truth. Sometimes you will feel lost and alone as you come into the new realms, but that is only because you are trying to equate yourselves with past time. Leave those past times alone – walk forward, because the walking forward is your purpose. The emotional detachments may leave you with strange feelings and yet true compassion and love can at last be shared.

All of you have all the answers within. You have the biggest library, the biggest computer, the biggest source of information within, because you have, as part of you, that droplet of the original godhead, and each droplet knows what every other droplet is doing, where they are and what they are shaping.

The most important thing to remember is: listen to your own hearts. There are changes, you and your planet are changing and this necessitates changes to what you consider to be structures, but in reality are not structures. In reality, everything flows, everything is active. Try to stagnate any activity and you will come up against enormous resistance, because you are resisting the flow of life. Yes, your globe will change its rhythm, its time and its place, as you understand it. Yes, other globes in your home that you call the solar system will change, and yes, this will change the way you feel and perceive, and actually change the physical experience. We cannot give you a time because we have none and as you come into a timeless zone, nor do you. We could say: very soon. But what is 'very soon'? Its magnetic pull has already changed, setting in place a different dance in the heavens. So be it. It is not important other than in observation. Your whole system is already moving differently and the majority of you will physically see some movement and shifts in your lifetime. The pattern of the kaleidoscope moves, we cannot say where that pattern will be at any given place or time, because within our scope of reality, there is no time. The shift energies shift constantly, that is all.

You now experience many things, which are neither right nor wrong. For some the experience is there to do, so will be done. The communication of different energies once made can never be unbroken, even if it is forgotten. There are many areas of vortices, they are not limited to one place. There are areas that are more conducive to the communication of different elements, spirits, different essences of life to which you all belong. Enjoy this, if that is what pleases you. Enjoy the communication, let it touch your own heart, open your heart. Listen to your true heart and you will understand that you can have true communication with all beings of light, wherever you live, wherever you are. Enjoy whatever you do.

If you take one drop of water and fill it with the energy of your heart, you will have the perfect medicine. The separation of the molecules is part of the experience but all you need is within one. That is the truth. If someone perceives something, it goes out into the mass consciousness. Water is life on your planet and it is important for your physical growth. If you follow the flow of water it will give you great inspiration. Everything mirrors everything else and water is a reflective element. It has much to teach you. Its properties are great on the physical being, the absorption of minerals within its molecules are refined in some places – it is very difficult to explain to you when you see what you consider to be dirt or pollution which is equated with evil. It is very difficult for us then to say, this is not evil, this is just another facet of everything else. However, if you register the pollution – which you see as evil – as part of you, as part of light, you transcend the disease that you feel it brings but you need to know this within the core of your being. Not guess, nor think, nor idealise, but know it. When you know, you can transcend what you consider to be evil, because evil is really another reflection of yourselves. This does not mean that you should not cherish your planet. In loving your planet you will never get pollution. That is all.

Chapter 13

The Union of Spirit and Matter

The crown centre, as you understand it, is your link to the divine. This is not inaccurate but as the shifting, moving consciousness expands, so your crown centre is able to accommodate all aspects of the world and the universe, letting in the light of different frequencies, in different times and different places. You therefore are becoming a multi-dimensional being.

You are familiar with these words but you do not fully understand what they mean. A multi-dimensional being is one who has no particular shape or form. This could manifest in the strangest of material shapes and different forms, both physical and spiritual. You understand it more as a spiritual form but now your world is able to accommodate this multi-dimensional state within your framework, so sparks of light fill and stimulate your whole head area. Not just opening your brain and your mind, but putting you in contact with the symmetry and the patterns of the cosmos. This you have experienced personally. This cannot be imagined although it can be realised without experience. But realising it without the experience means very little – it can only present an echo of the real state.

The real state is the ability to be all or nothing – to be part of all and nothing and yet still live within the framework of your body. This perhaps best illustrates what we have tried to put across. The importance is the communication, the connection and the amalgamation of spirit and matter. So your head centre at this point does not just open but clears completely. There is no doorway, no entry point. It just is. You just become. Again these words, for some, will be realised but not recognised as an actuality. However, the echo of that actuality itself is an important lead to what now is possible.

We therefore ask you all: why bother with those things around you that are so unimportant? We do not mean for you to give up your responsibility of the matter-state. What we say is: live within the matter-state and get on with what needs to be done today. Do not be drawn away by those stories and tales of greater knowledge and expansion when really, dear children, that knowledge is within you. It is not wrong to be drawn away by things that seem incredible or amazing, but it serves no purpose whatsoever in your true understanding of the cosmos, because it only presents to you a tiny part of the picture, and this tiny part of the picture does not help you to see the whole.

These are times when it is fascinating to look at some detail of life, at some energies, and you now know that many different energies exist. But energies in themselves, wherever they are, whatever form or shape they take, are all part of the whole cosmos, the picture of which is enormous. It has shapes beyond your strangest dreams. We have had to do some work on the channeller and her experiences have been important to allow the accommodation of this information. We emphasise this is not a special state for her or for anyone because that special state is within all of you.

There is no special person, you are all special people, because each one of you, each tiny fragment of energy, is of great worth and it is only now that you can realise this as an actuality, not just as a concept. Only when you realise it as an actuality do you truly understand what we are impressing upon you. The words that we have used are specifically to help you when these things begin to occur in actualisation – for you to understand that you are safe, that what you feel and know is truly right. You cannot know through the words we give; you can read the words with interest. You can sometimes even feel the energy that comes through with the words, but you cannot understand by the words alone. At best, they mirror and reflect the cosmos, but they cannot teach you. Only when your individual experience allows, will you fully understand. It is time to give these words, because, one by one, you are becoming enlightened, and as you are you will remember the words you have read, and will realise their true meaning.

Every corner and part of the cosmos is cherished. You speak, in your terms, of a drop in the ocean, and each drop, wherever it lands, even the dark drops – as you understand darkness – are loved. They are cherished and are part of the enormous pattern that goes into the cosmos. This pattern is not static, it is moving all the time. You do not exactly see them, but changes happen all the time. Whole galaxies dissolve and whole galaxies are born. Everything that is dissolved becomes something else. Your own physical planet has itself been part of other planets, it has been part of a sun, it has evolved and transmuted, and the consciousness energy of your planet is now moving. Those of you who are sensitive enough to grasp this can lock into the earth's energy and realise its force, its rumbling, deep force. When you feel this deep force, it is nothing to the force that is in operation in the cosmos of which you are part. It is easy to feel insignificant, everything that moves has energy. The movement is an energetic force of expansion, this is why the movement of yourselves – not as physical entities, but as spiritual truths – is of utmost importance at this time, because the movement of your consciousness is equivalent to the energy of the biggest explosion.

That energy of rising consciousness affects the patterns, the turning wheels of all that you know and more. Now do you understand what we mean when we say your purpose is to be? When you fully comprehend this, as an actualisation, you become rather like an enormous flame and your energy is such that the flame is alive, and far from being a destroying, dissolving flame, it is a flame of building matter. This flame of building matter will create a new consciousness-globe, a new consciousness in the universe, a new pattern, a new colour, a new shape – and a new experience so that every part of the cosmos benefits by that exploration.

Now where does your darkness come into all this? What is negativity? What is fear? Darkness is just part of the experience. It is not evil, it is the experience of that particular frequency that has been chosen by those who experience it, no matter what pain is involved. The pain is part of that choice, and when the experience has been taken, the experience echoes in the cosmos – your fears of a take-over of the negative forces are incorrect, the negative forces as you understand them are a tiny part of the pattern, giving colour to the whole. Those who are stuck in the three-dimensional state will not understand this, seeing only the pain, the suffering and the evil. But when you start to grow, when you begin to see an overview, you begin to look at this negativity in a different light. Not condoning it, but recognising it as the true experience that it is, and then, because of that knowledge, you will never have to experience negativity again because you see it as it is and it holds no fear for you.

Even with the darkness that healers sometimes see, the evil darkness that permeates individuals like a dark cloud, even that will be released when the individual and the negative energy realise the experience of that particular time, that particular pain. Indeed the suffering, the pain and the darkness will only be released by the owner's transcendental movement.

Do not therefore be caught up by the anguish of others' pain, rather reveal to them, by your being, that enlightenment and joy are possible. You see darkness as something to be ignored, or something to be dealt with as quickly as possible. Pain and suffering have been needed for the human experience. There is no other place in the cosmos that has had your kind of physical pain. It has been a heavy load but it has been one that you have chosen. We have all chosen. Sometimes in the darkest misery people say that their god has deserted them. Yet they are the god and they are not deserted.

The opening of the crown centre will reveal new stars, new consciousness, new growth, and the crown fully opened to the higher intuitive knowing state is in absolute place within your being.

You will now be able to communicate this through your throat centre, not necessarily through words, but you will be able to draw the openness of true light and enlightenment into the communication states: the energy of love as it manifests in the heart, the energy of compassion as you truly sympathise with others, the energy of power as you come into your own empowerment, and the energy of human physical matter as you experience your life and your world with its own many patterns, energies and forces.

So through realisation from the opening of the crown centre all of your being in every area will radiate with the purpose of the loving, open fluid state of enlightenment. You see the cosmos as myriad patterns, you see the cosmos in high colours, some of which you do not recognise. All these colours are a facet of the light and the light is made manifest through your hearts, into your state of being. That is why your heart and love are a cherished energy, not just on your planet, but in the whole cosmos, because the light-force joins to matter creating the desire of true love.

Do not be complacent, do not involve yourselves with pettiness of groups and societies whose only interest is something of a performance, something that has an excitement, but will really only cloak you from the whole of your being. Communicate with people, communicate with everything, not just your fellow man but all the energies in your earth, above and below and in-between. You can communicate with all these energies by the knowledge, the openness, and the realisation of the light-force made manifest within your own hearts. That is all.

Over the last few years you have seen many words

written, or heard channelled experiences, but these channellings will begin to be very much fewer because the need of the echo becomes unnecessary. When the realisation takes place, some channelled words will not be conducive to you because that particular frequency reveals itself in a way that you will not be able to acknowledge.

Note that we carefully choose not to say that anything is wrong! Nothing is wrong, but everything, and every word spoken must echo the voice of true love and wonderment in your heart, not as an extraordinary piece of information in your mind – that is nothing. Anyone can create these things. But the words must echo in your heart otherwise they have no meaning whatsoever. You must discern from them that which is truly correct for you. Do not be attached to channelled predictions. There cannot be accurate predictions because the pattern of the cosmos is fluid. How can time be measured by a higher consciousness when the higher consciousness knows the irrelevance of time?

When you are caught up in your lives, in the particular colours of your particular patterns of experience, you experience time on your planet as a continuous absolute state: twenty-four hours in your day, sixty seconds in your minute. But it has never been that way. You measure time, but it is not a reality. The reason you have felt that time has speeded up is because you are beginning to understand, as a realised state, that time does not exist. You are timeless beings but your planet is being drawn into a new shape, a new pattern, new colour, new sound, and this drawing is slowing the trajectory of your universe. This is the only way we can explain your 'time'.

Every individual experiences time differently and if you

got ten people to sit and concentrate for one of your minutes, each one of those individuals would experience that time-span in a different way. Man believes himself to be clever in the measurement of those things that cannot be measured, but the measurement of the turning of wheels has been part of the desired experience that you understand as karma. By experiencing karma – which is the giving and receiving, the cause and the effect – by living out a physical actuality, you live out the dance of the cosmos in all its splendour.

As your conscious awareness shifts and, therefore, the connection with the physical state becomes less important, the energy of the individual is, if you like, excited by this, and that excitement creates movement. It is through that movement that the acceleration of experience appears to occur. Time is a fluid element, but it needed to be realised in its human state – in its karmic state – to create the experiences that you needed. You are, however, coming out of that experience, therefore time changes and it feels very much to you as though there is no time. You have an expression that time runs away, but if you take your thoughts out into the cosmos, you will see that within the revolving wheels of your particular tiny part of the cosmos, it is, at this moment, being drawn into a new shape and pattern which, as you understand it, is time slowing down. So perhaps the simplest thing to say is that, although you feel time is speeding up, it is not correct. However you need not worry about this – you all have plenty of time!

Try to allow all of this in without continually asking questions, for when there are no questions there is stillness, and only when your questions cease do you truly understand. Man's greatest attribute is his curiosity.

That curiosity was part of his experience, and through his curiosity he has had a myriad of experiences. It is quite right to question, but when you rise up to a level of understanding beyond the third dimension all your questions dissolve into light, because it is the manifestation of light in all of its many, many guises and patterns that is the truth.

There is a star above you now. You have cherished and worshipped this star as your sun, and this star-consciousness embraces all that you are because in a sense, it is your guardian. It has nurtured you. It has cherished you as its own children. This star is moving, growing, radiating from that greater understanding which comes, in part, from you and from all upon the globe called Earth.

That sun, that star, is in constant communication with other stars and they communicate their experience. It is fascinating that with your ears in the third-dimensional state you could not hear the sound of that communication, but some have heard the echo of this and experienced the wonder and the joy of realising that all and everything is in communication with each other.

When you worry about your tiny part of the enormous cosmos, your perspective is low and you see very little. But as you begin to reach up, you can talk to your sun and be part of that star, and in turn you can be part of the communication of the whole cosmos.

Understand the joy of communication, the joy of experience, the joy of being wherever you are. Whatever shape you have chosen to take, whatever colour you radiate, you are a joy to the whole, to all of us. Therefore en-joy yourselves.